From The Library
of
Robert A. Cospito

LEGAL-WISE®

LEGAL-WISE®

Carl W. Battle

Attorney-at-Law

ALLWORTH PRESS, NEW YORK

Published by Allworth Press, an imprint of
Allworth Communications, Inc., 10 East 23rd Street, New York, NY 10010.

Distributor to the trade in the United States:
Consortium Book Sales & Distribution, Inc.
287 East Sixth Street, Suite 365
Saint Paul, MN 55101.

Distributor to the trade in Canada:
Raincoast Books Distribution Limited
112 East 3rd Avenue
Vancouver, B.C. V5t 1C8.

Book design by Douglas Design Associates, New York, NY.

LEGAL-WISE® is a registered trademark of National Legal Information Services, Philadelphia, Pennsylvania.

To my wife, Dyan, who always inspires me.

Table of Contents

Preface 11

Chapter 1   **Managing Your Legal Affairs**
            • Your Participation in the American Legal System
            • Your Right to Represent Yourself.. 13

Chapter 2   **Finding The Best Lawyer for You**
            • Which Lawyer Is Right for You? • Using the Sample Attorney's Retainer
            Agreement • Form: Attorney's Retainer Agreement............................ 15

Chapter 3   **Preparing Your Will**
            • What Is a Will? • Requirements of a Valid Will • Intent to Make a Will
            • Capacity to Make a Will • Signing Your Will • The Witnesses to Your Will
            • Using the Sample Will Form • Other Clauses for Your Will
            • Revoking Your Will • Checklist for Preparing Your Will • Form: Last Will
            And Testament • Sample Clauses for Wills • Form: Codicil...................... 21

Chapter 4   **Easy Steps to Probate a Will**
            • Definition of Probate • Procedures for Probating an Estate
            • Petition/Application to Probate a Will • Checklist for Filing Petition/
            Application for Probate • Form: Petition/Application to Probate Will........ 29

Chapter 5   **Using a Living Trust to Avoid Probate**
            • Making Use of a Living Trust • Understanding the Trust Agreement
            • Checklist for Establishing a Living Trust • Form: Trust Agreement............ 33

Chapter 6   **Making a Living Will**
            • The Functions of a Living Will • Checklist for Making a Living Will
            • Form: Living Will 37

Chapter 7   **How to Make an Organ Donor Pledge**
            • Making a Gift of Your Body or Organ
            • Form: Pledge of Human Body, Organ, or Part Thereof 41

Chapter 8 **Transferring Your Personal Rights by an Assignment**
• What Is an Assignment? • What Rights Are Assignable? • Requirements for
Making a Valid Assignment • Using the Sample Assignment Form
• Form: Assignment 43

Chapter 9 **Operating through Someone Else by Power of Attorney**
• Understanding the Power of Attorney • Requirements for Making a
Power of Attorney • Form: Power of Attorney 47

Chapter 10 **Buying and Selling Your Home**
• Understanding Real Estate Sales • Using a Real Estate Agent • Making a
Real Estate Agreement of Sale • Obtaining Financing for Your Real Estate
Purchase • What Happens at Closing? • Checklist for Sale or Purchase of
Real Estate • Form: Real Estate Listing Agreement • Form: Real Estate
Agreement of Sale • Form: Promissory Note • Form: General Warranty Deed
• Form: Special Warranty Deed • Form: Quitclaim Deed........................... 51

Chapter 11 **Leasing Your Home or Office**
• Looking at Renting • Understanding Landlord-Tenant Law
• Types of Landlord-Tenant Relationships • Warranty of Habitability
• Other Landlord-Tenant Obligations • Security Deposits • Assignment and
Subletting • Basic Provisions of a Lease Agreement • Checklist for Making a
Lease • Form: Lease Agreement.. 67

Chapter 12 **Personal Property for Sale**
• Buying and Selling Personal Property • Form: Bill of Sale 77

Chapter 13 **Contracting for Repairs and Services**
• Entering into a Contract for Services • Form: Contract for Services 81

Chapter 14 **Handling a Simple Divorce or Separation**
• What to Do When Relationships Don't Work • Property Settlement and Other
Agreements • Going Though a Divorce • Checklist for Filing a Simple Divorce
• Form: Property Settlement Agreement • Form: Complaint for Divorce
• Form: Affidavit of Consent 85

Chapter 15 **Getting a New Name**
• What's in a Name? • Changing Your Name • Checklist for Filing Petition to
Change Name • Form: Petition to Change Name • Form: Petition to Change
Name of Minor Child • Form: Consent to Name Change 95

Chapter 16 **Being Successful in Small Claims Court**
• Knowing about Small Claims Court • Should You Go to Court?
• Bringing Your Case in Court • Using Affidavits to Prove Your Case
• Winning and Collecting a Judgment • Checklist for Bringing a Civil
Case in Court • Form: Civil Complaint • Form: Affidavit 103

Chapter 17   **Using Releases to Settle Legal Claims**
• Releasing Someone from a Claim • Form: Release 113

Chapter 18   **Patenting and Marketing Your Ideas and Inventions**
• What Do You Do with Your Ideas? • Can You Protect Your Idea? • Where Can You Go for Help? • Patent Attorneys and Agents • Invention Promotion Firms • Invention Brokers • University Invention/ Entrepreneurial Centers • The Small Business Administration • National Bureau of Standards • Inventor's Clubs/Associations/Societies • What Is a Patent? • Conception and Reduction to Practice • What Is a Patentable Invention? • Who May Apply for a Patent? • Application for Patent • Oath or Declaration and Signature • Filing Fees • Specification: a) Title of Invention; b) Cross References to Related Applications; c) Background of the Invention; d) Summary of the Invention; e) Description of the Drawings; f) Detailed Description; g) Patent Claims; h) Abstract of the Disclosure i) Drawing • Examination of Applications in the Patent and Trademark Office • Infringement of Patents • Checklist for Filing a U.S. Patent Application • Form: Transmittal Form for a U.S. Patent Application • Form: Declaration Claiming Small Entity Status • Form: Declaration for Patent Application • Form: List of Art Cited by Applicant • Form: Nondisclosure Agreement 117

Chapter 19   **Use and Registration of Trademarks**
• Function of Trademarks • Registration of Trademarks • Filing a Trademark Application • International Classification of Goods and Services • Checklist for Registering a Trademark • Form: Trademark/Service Mark Application 137

Chapter 20   **Copyrights to Your Writings and Artistic Works**
• Introducing You to Copyrights • Subject Matter of Copyright Protection • Copyright Notice • Registering Your Copyright • Checklist for Registering a Copyright • Form: Application Form TX • Form: Application Form SR • Form: Application Form PA • Form: Application Form VA 145

Chapter 21   **Obtaining Debt Relief Through Bankruptcy**
• Deciding to File for Bankruptcy • Filing under Chapter 7 — Liquidation • Filing Fee • The Chapter 7 Bankruptcy Petition • Exempt Property • Filing under Chapter 13 — Adjustment of Debts • Filing Requirements under Chapter 13 • The Chapter 13 Bankruptcy Petition • Fraudulent Transfers • Receiving a Discharge from Your Debts • Non-Dischargeable Debts • Checklist for Filing for Bankruptcy • Form: Application to Pay Filing Fee in Installments (Form No. 3) • Form: Debtor's Petition (Form No.1) • Form: Debtors' Joint Petition (Form No. 2) • Form: Statement of Assets and Liabilities (Form No. 6) • Form: Statement of Financial Affairs for Debtor Not Engaged in Business (Form No. 7) • Form: Schedule of Current Income and Current Expenditures (Form No. 6A) • Form: Chapter 13 Statement (Form No. 10) • Form: Chapter 13 Plan • List of Creditors, with Addresses 159

Chapter 22 **Helping You in an IRS Audit**
• Dealing with the IRS • The Audit Process: 1) Selection of Returns; 2) Audit of Your Tax Return; 3) Notification of an Audit; 4) What Happens During an IRS Audit; 5) Repetitive Audits • Appealing an IRS Audit • Protest Letter Requirements • The Collection of Unpaid Taxes • Some Useful IRS Publications 195

Appendix Sources of Additional Information 201

Index 203

Preface

We live in an extremely complex society, and our interactions with other people and with countless institutions are becoming even more complex. If there is any doubt about the validity of this observation, you need only consider that ours is the most litigious society in the world. With this in mind, it has become clear that the protection and enforcement of individual rights, the need to solve disputes and the management of legal affairs, are rapidly becoming the routine concerns of each and every one of us.

It is a deeply-rooted principle in American law that "ignorance of the law is no excuse." Therefore, it is imperative that you have a basic understanding of law to protect your legal rights and interests and to conduct your legal affairs properly.

Renting an apartment? Buying your first home? Thinking about a will? Starting your own business? This book was designed for your use with these questions and many others in mind. While not designed to replace in any way the advice and services of a lawyer, *LEGAL-WISE®* is a self-help guide dedicated to the proposition that the information revolution has finally reached the courthouse and the lawyer's office.

Included here are detailed and easy-to-follow forms, instructions and advice for individual representation in areas such as wills, leases, copyrights, patents, trademarks, small claims court, name changes, divorce, bankruptcy, and IRS audits — each accompanied by a concise and lucid presentation of the relevant laws and rules. Other forms and discussions explain how to close on your house, make an assignment, prepare a power of attorney, and contract for repairs and services, and several other very useful and potentially expense-saving procedures.

The idea here is to put together in a simple, non-threatening form the kinds of things you might need in your daily life. This book should provide you with a basic familiarity with the laws, legal forms and procedures such that you can manage your simple legal affairs, or make an informed decision to seek appropriate legal counsel. This book also provides in many cases an estimated cost for typical legal services if you decide you need a lawyer.

The second edition of *LEGAL-WISE® Self-Help Legal Forms for Everyone* reflects important changes in the law since the original publication in 1985 and adds some helpful new topics. As the laws are constantly changing, you are advised to check with the court clerk or an attorney in your jurisdiction for new developments. The sample forms and instructions in this book are appropriate for most, if not all, states and jurisdictions. You can typically call or write your court clerk for specific court rules and requirements.

11

1 *Managing Your Legal Affairs*

Your Participation in the American Legal System

Do you have faith in the American legal system? A large number of people would probably answer this question negatively. Despite a lack of public confidence, the American legal system is perhaps the best in the world.

Although it suffers from many problems and inequities, our legal system is a remarkable one. Our judicial and legislative processes are structured to safeguard individual interests and freedoms, while concurrently protecting the interests of society in general. This requires a delicate balance in many cases, but it is a task which our system is clearly capable of handling. Our country has a well-trained and active judiciary. Our legal profession has an abundance of talent and resources. The major weakness in our legal system, however, is the absence of public awareness and participation.

Our legal system is an active one, and, unlike that of many countries, it truly has the capacity for justice. However, it desperately needs an active involvement by the public. It needs a public desirous of being knowledgeable in the law. It needs a public willing to monitor, evaluate, and formulate policies in American law. Further, it needs public confidence and support. American democracy cannot long live without the will of the people. Likewise, the American legal system cannot, and will not, function effectively without *you*.

There are perhaps no areas having such widespread and daily effects on American life as law. Laws regulate your family relationships, commercial activities and your social conduct. Although protected by individual liberties under the U.S. Constitution, Americans are a heavily regulated people.

The laws regulating American society do not necessarily represent a destruction of individual rights. Many of the laws were enacted for the very purpose of protecting such rights. The protection of the law is generally lost, however, because of public unawareness and mismanagement of legal affairs. Because an unwanted lawsuit or loss of important legal rights can destroy fortunes, families, and lives, you need to manage your legal affairs as routinely and carefully as you balance your checkbook. The magic formula is simply knowing your legal rights, knowing how to enforce them, and knowing how to reduce important legal transactions to writing. A written document, such as a contract, a deed, or a will can be extremely important as evidence of your legal rights and obligations. Never rely on oral promises or a handshake to protect your rights.

Most people have no understanding of how the legal system operates and how cases are won or lost in court. You should find time to sit in on some court cases to see firsthand how the court functions. Court proceedings are typically open to the public.

Serving as a juror on a civil or criminal trial is another excellent means to see how the legal system works.

Your Right to Represent Yourself
More and more people are starting to take the law into their own hands. People are becoming hungry for information about law and self-help legal material. The 1980's and 90's will be remembered as the era of self-help. Many people are taking the do-it-yourself route in auto repairs, carpentry, home improvements, and many other areas. You also need to take the self-help approach in handling your simple legal affairs. Hiring a lawyer simply is not necessary for many of your routine legal matters.

The right to represent yourself is a basic concept of federal constitutional law. Although this right is nowhere spelled out in the Constitution, its existence is recognized by the courts as fundamental to our system of individual liberties. However, the right to represent yourself is not advantageous unless you have knowledge of the law. This includes knowing how to prepare legal forms and other documents, as well as how to safeguard and enforce legal rights.

Moreover, knowledge of the law encourages more public participation in the legal system. It eliminates the dependence that people have on lawyers in handling legal matters. Also, if you are familiar with the law, you will be better able to monitor a lawyer's work if you need to hire one.

Some areas of law can be very complex and may require the services of a good lawyer. But, to the extent that you can, try to represent yourself in your simple legal matters. You may consider consulting with an attorney only for guidance as you prepare to handle the matter yourself.

2 Finding the Best Lawyer for You

Which Lawyer Is Right for You?

With the complexities of life and the laws governing us, the need for competent and effective legal advice arises on many occasions. Finding a good lawyer who is right for you and your particular situation can sometimes be difficult. There are, however, several sources you can use in helping you locate good legal counsel.

In searching for a good lawyer, you should use your personal contacts, local bar associations, telephone directories, legal publications, and community organizations. Each of these may be a good source of information and assistance in obtaining the right lawyer. Your final selection of a lawyer should involve an analysis of your specific facts, the complexity of your case, and the character and experience of the individual lawyer.

Unquestionably, the best approach for you in choosing a suitable lawyer is through personal contacts with relatives, friends, and business associates. Relatives and friends who have had similar legal matters satisfactorily handled can recommend their own personal lawyers. Such recommendations are the truest measure of a lawyer's reputation and zeal. Moreover, relatives and friends will generally have your best interests at heart and are less likely to do a disservice in referring you to a lawyer.

Local bar associations usually maintain a lawyer referral service which can be employed in directing you to appropriate legal counsel. Specific information on these services can be obtained by calling or writing to the bar association in your area. They are usually listed in the telephone directory under "Association" or "Professional Organization." The referral services typically involve a brief telephone discussion with a lawyer, who reviews the general facts and refers you to one or more lawyers handling such cases.

Although this service does help in narrowing your search for the proper lawyer, it gives little aid in measuring a lawyer's eagerness, character, and integrity. All lawyers are required to meet the standards of the Code of Professional Responsibility, such as zealously representing you, safeguarding your confidential discussions, and providing competent legal services. You need to find a lawyer who measures up to these standards.

As a supplement to their referral services, the bar associations in many cities provide taped lectures over the telephone. This is a good program for providing some basic legal information to the public. The taped lectures usually run from five to fifteen minutes, and cover a variety of subjects such as criminal law, divorce, landlord/tenant relationships, and much more. The law tapes can be a valuable resource for helping you understand your legal problems and make informed decisions to seek legal advice. You can usually find these services in the telephone directory under such names as

"Lawline", "TeleLaw" or the like. Also, you can generally contact your bar association for information on these law tapes.

As you can see, your local telephone directory is a very good source to use in locating a lawyer. The "Yellow Pages," in particular, gives an extensive listing of lawyers and law firms. These can typically be found under the heading of "Attorneys" or "Lawyers." Many Yellow Pages listings present basic information such as telephone numbers, office hours, fee schedules, and areas of concentration.

Legal directories, publications, and community organizations are additional sources for help in finding a lawyer. Many large urban areas have directories of lawyers, which often give information on both educational background and training. Legal magazines and newspapers frequently carry articles and advertisements by and about lawyers which may be useful to you. Community organizations such as neighborhood centers, local chapters of the American Civil Liberties Union, legal aid societies, law school clinical programs, consumer agencies, and tenants associations can also be excellent references.

In many areas, legal services plans can provide relatively inexpensive legal services for monthly membership fees of about $10-20. Legal services plans typically provide a list of plan lawyers who are available to you for handling some simple, routine legal matters at no additional cost. Examples of some normal services are the following:

- legal consultation and advice in person, by phone or mail during normal business hours;

- legal letters and phone calls on your behalf;

- preparation of a simple will;

- review of documents, such as leases, real estate papers, contracts, etc., up to a specified number of pages;

- advice in representing yourself in small claims court;

- advice on your rights under government programs, such as Social Security and Veteran's Programs; and

- emergency bail service.

Check the telephone directory for legal services plans which may be available in your area.

Legal clinics can also be a source for relatively inexpensive routine legal services. These clinics usually handle high volumes of simple cases such as bankruptcies, wills, uncontested divorces, personal injuries and many others.

Your search for legal counsel should always focus on finding the right lawyer for you. This necessarily will involve an evaluation of many factors, such as the lawyer's reputation, experience, loyalty, personality and fees. You should always choose a lawyer that you can afford and trust.

You should try to find a lawyer who is experienced in handling cases such as yours. This is especially true in cases involving complex areas such as taxes, patents, malpractice, immigration, commercial activities, and other specialized areas.

It is important that you find out as much as possible about a lawyer before retaining him or her. Explore the lawyer's reputation in the community and with former clients. Is the lawyer honest and loyal to clients? Is the lawyer responsible and conscientious about his or her work? To assist you in answering these questions, ask the lawyer for references and then contact them to investigate the lawyer's reputation. It is important that you review and understand fully all financial aspects of your case with your lawyer. You should get information on the lawyer's fees, witness fees, court costs and other charges in writing from the lawyer in advance. Avoid lawyers who are unwilling to discuss fees and charges up front. Try to get the lawyer to handle your case on a contingency basis, if possible. On this basis, you only pay your lawyer a percentage (typically one third) of your actual recovery. Lawyers typically handle accidents, personal injury, property damage, collections and some estate cases on a contingency fee basis.

You should review the merits of your case with the lawyer in detail. He or she should be willing to explain the legal issues and procedures to you. Watch out for lawyers who guarantee to win your case for you. Although a lawyer may be able to give you an estimated probability of success, he or she cannot ensure the outcome in any case. If you have done your homework, by becoming generally familiar with the law, you will be better able to monitor the lawyer's work. All too often, however, people retain lawyers in complete ignorance of their legal rights and remedies, and with no understanding of what the lawyer is to do. There is no substitute for an informed client in ensuring proper integrity and performance by a lawyer.

Using the Sample Attorney's Retainer Agreement

When hiring a lawyer, be sure to enter into a written retainer agreement. A sample Attorney's Retainer Agreement is provided at the end of this chapter. Item 1 of the sample Attorney's Retainer Agreement should be filled in by giving the date, the client's name and address, and the lawyer's name and office address. Item 1 should also describe as completely as possible the transaction or matter for which legal representation is sought.

Item 2 should include a complete listing of the duties and services the lawyer is to perform. This can become a handy checklist for gauging the lawyer's performance.

Item 3 should set forth the manner in which you will pay the lawyer for legal services. This should include amounts, payment dates, and all other terms and conditions regarding payment of legal fees. The agreement may provide for a retainer or flat fee to be paid to the lawyer for han-

dling the entire matter. Many times, the retainer is only a first payment or advance against an hourly or contingency fee. Alternately, provisions can be made to pay the lawyer an hourly rate, with the lawyer providing an accounting for his or her time. Also, the lawyer may accept payment on a contingency arrangement based on a certain percentage of any funds received.

Payment for costs and expenses such as court fees, filing fees, witness fees, long distance telephone calls, travel, copying of documents, and investigative services should be provided for in item 4. Generally, the client pays for these costs, but agreement may be made otherwise. In any event, try to obtain a good faith estimate of these costs from your lawyer and list them in item 4. You should require that the lawyer obtain your approval before incurring any costs and expenses greater than some specified amount.

Item 5 provides that you can terminate your attorney retainer agreement at any time and for any reason. Your lawyer can terminate the agreement for valid cause, such as your noncooperation or nonpayment, or with your consent. In any event, termination of the agreement should not be allowed when it would harm or prejudice your case.

Item 6 provides for the immediate refund of the money paid to your lawyer if the agreement is terminated; except that you and your lawyer may agree to deduct payment for time, costs, and expenses from your refund or credit.

Item 7 obligates your lawyer to give you or any new attorney a copy of all documents in your file at your request. Any additional terms that you or your lawyer may have can be added to Item 8.

The agreement should be signed by both you and your lawyer. It is also recommended that the Attorney's Retainer Agreement, as well as any other agrements or documents used from this book, be initialed and dated on each page to prevent fraud and substitution of pages. You should keep a copy for your records.

Attorney's Retainer Agreement

1. This is an Agreement made as of the _____ day of _____, 19____, between

(Client's name)_____,

(Client's address)_____._

(hereinafter referred to as the "Client") and

(Attorney's name)_____,

(Attorney's address)_____,

(hereinafter referred to as the "Lawyer"), which defines the terms and conditions under which Client has retained Lawyer to provide legal counsel and services relating to the following matter:

_____

_____

_____

_____

_____(hereinafter referred to as "Client's Case").

2. Lawyer agrees to provide competent legal counsel and services to Client in connection with Client's Case and to perform the services provided below:

_____

_____

_____

_____

3. In consideration for the legal counsel and services performed by Lawyer, Client agrees to make payment to Lawyer as follows:

_____

_____

_____

_____

4. a) Client agrees to pay all reasonable costs and expenses incurred by Lawyer in connection with Client's Case. Lawyer estimates in good faith that these costs are as follows:

_____

_____

_____

b) Lawyer agrees to obtain Client's prior approval before incurring any costs and any other expenses on behalf of Client in an amount greater than $_____.

5. Client has the right to terminate this Agreement at any time at Client's discretion. Lawyer may terminate this agreement for valid cause upon Client's consent, provided that Client's Case is not prejudiced or harmed thereby.

6. Upon termination of this Agreement, Client shall be entitled to the immediate refund or credit of all amounts paid or due, except as provided below:

_____

_____

_____

_____

7. After termination of this Agreement, Lawyer agrees to provide to any new attorney or to Client, upon Client's request, a copy of all documents which Lawyer has possession of relating to Client's Case.

8. Additional terms and conditions:

Client and Lawyer, intending to be legally bound, have signed this Agreement on the date first indicated above.

_____   _____
Client's signature   Lawyer's signature

Chapter

3 *Preparing Your Will*

What Is a Will?

A will is a legal document which is prepared with certain formalities and under which you direct what will happen to your property after your death. Your will is effective only upon your death and it can be modified or revoked by you at any time during your life. If you should die without leaving a will, your property will be distributed according to state law and will generally go to your spouse and children or other next of kin.

There are several good reasons why you should prepare a will. Your will expresses your specific wishes as to how you want your property distributed and it eliminates speculation and confusion about how your estate will be given away. Also, it states who you want to handle your estate and can identify who you would want as guardian of any minor children. Equally important, your will provides a good inventory of your property and assets. Without this, it may be difficult for someone to identify and locate any real estate, bank accounts, safe deposit boxes, securities, or other personal property you may have in various places. Preparing your will is also good because it causes you to seriously consider the extent of your property, family, and friends and to plan your estate accordingly.

Before making your will, you should prepare a list of all of your real and personal property. This list should be complete with all your real estate, bank accounts, safe de-posit boxes, stocks and bonds, automobiles, furniture, jewelry, artwork and all other assets. It is also good to list any insurance policies you may have, even though insurance proceeds will generally be paid directly to the beneficiary named in the policy. You should also prepare a list of your children, spouse, other family members, friends, charities and others which you would like to make beneficiaries in your will. Next, you should prepare a distribution plan which shows how you want your property distributed among your family, friends and others. Identify someone that you would like to name as Executor (male) or Executrix (female) to carry out your wishes and the distribution of your estate. You should also identify an alternate person in the event that the first Executor or Executrix is unable to serve. With all the information you have just gathered, you can now prepare your will.

Requirements of a Valid Will

The formal requirements for making a valid will depend on state law. However, most, if not all, of the states recognize four general requirements in the formation of a valid will. First, there must be the necessary intent to make a will. This means that you must intend for the document and the words contained therein to operate as your will upon your death. Secondly, you must be of legal age and have the legal capacity to make a will. This means that you must have actual knowledge of the act that you are performing. You must also have an understanding of your property and your relationship to others at the time of making your will. Third, your will must be made free of fraud, duress, undue influence and mistake. Fourth, your will must be executed in accordance with the formal requirements of your state law. This generally requires that your will be signed by you and by two disinterested witnesses in the presence of each other. Some states may require that the will be witnessed by three people. Therefore, it is recommended that you have at least three people sign your will as witnesses.

Intent to Make a Will
A valid will generally requires that you, as the maker, have the intent to make a will. This is a question of fact which is determined from the circumstances surrounding the making of your will. Where your will is a sham or was executed as a joke, the required testamentary intent is lacking and your will is invalid. If you prepare a document or agreement which shows an intent to make a will in the future, this document or agreement is not a valid will. For your will to be valid, it must show your present intent to make a will.

Capacity to Make a Will
For the required testamentary capacity to make a will, you must be of legal age and sound mental capacity. The legal age in most states is 18 years. The sound mental capacity requires that you be able to (1) understand the relationship between you and the natural objects of your generosity, such as your spouse, children, and other family members; (2) understand the nature and extent of your property; and (3) understand that you are executing your will. The required mental capacity must exist at the time that you make your will. If you should later lose the required mental capacity, this does not affect the validity of an earlier will executed when you did have the required mental capacity.

Your capacity to make a will can be influenced by alcohol, drugs, medications, illness, and mental disease. To help avoid questions about your capacity to make a will, your will should contain an introductory clause declaring that you are of sound mind and body, have full testamentary intent and capacity, and voluntarily execute that document as your last will and testament. Your will should also include a witness attestation clause in which the witnesses declare that you are of sound mind and body and signed of your free will.

Signing Your Will
The valid execution of your will requires that it be signed by you. Your signature generally must appear at the end of the will. However, it is recommended that you sign at the end of each page to prevent fraud and substitution of pages. You should use your regular and complete signature, although any name or mark used by you and intended as your signature is generally acceptable. You should sign your will in the presence of the witnesses who will be attesting to it. If you are unable to sign your will, generally you can have another person sign for you. This must be done in your presence and in the presence of the witnesses and be at your specific direction.

The Witnesses to Your Will
It is required that your will be witnessed by two or three people, depending on state law. This usually requires that the witnesses observe your signing and also sign the will themselves in your presence and the presence of each other.

Who may be a witness to your will is also governed by your state law. Generally, any competent person who is of legal age can be a witness. Some states require that the witnesses not be beneficiaries under the will or lose their gift under the will if they act as witnesses. Therefore, it is recommended that your will be witnesses by disinterested witnessed who will not be beneficiaries under your will.

Your will should contain a witness attestation clause which declares that the will was signed and published in their presence and that you were of sound mind and body and acting from your free will at that time. This witness attestation clause may be useful in preventing challenges to your will that might be based on arguments that you lacked testamentary intent and capacity.

Your witnesses should include their addresses along with their signatures so they will be easier to find. In some states, your will can be "self-proving" if your signature and that of your witnesses are notarized. If your will is "self-proving," your signature and your witnesses' signatures are presumed to be valid.

Using the Sample Will Form

A sample will form is provided at the end of this chapter for your use in preparing a simple will.

Clause 1 is a declaration that you are of sound mind and body and free will, that you have full testamentary intent and capacity, and that you voluntarily make your will.

In Clause 2 you include your current domicile.

Clause 3 is an express revocation of all wills and codicils previously executed by you. A codicil is an amendment to a will which does not revoke it, but merely modifies it. A sample codicil form is also provided at the end of this chapter. Note that a valid codicil must be prepared with the same requirements for making a valid will.

Clause 4 provides for the appointment of an Executor or Executrix for your estate. Your will should provide that no bond be required for the Executor or Executrix to carry out his or her duties in your will.

Clause 5 directs your Executor or Executrix to pay all of your just debts and other expenses of the administration of your estate. These debts and expenses are usually paid directly from the assets of your estate before any distribution is made to your beneficiaries.

In Clause 6 you provide for your gifts to the beneficiaries. In the simplest form these can be gifts of specific property to named individuals. You may also make gifts to members of a class, such as your children, brothers or sisters and the like. Care must be taken to make certain that any gift will vest within 21 years after the life of some specific person. For complicated will and trust provisions you should consult an attorney. Typical legal fees for preparing a simple will range from about $100 to about $300, depending on location.

In many states, your surviving spouse may be entitled to a certain minimum portion (usually from 1/4 to 1/2) of your estate regardless of what your will provides. Thus, you may need to indicate in your will whether any bequest or devise to your spouse is in lieu of, or in addition to, any minimum portion mandated by state law.

Likewise, some states provide that a child who is not mentioned or provided for in your will may be entitled to a share of your estate. Similar provisions may apply to children born after execution of your will. For these reasons, your state laws should be checked for specific provisions to testamentary gifts to children. It is recommended that all your children be acknowledged and mentioned in your will, even if you do not leave them anything or only leave a small token gift.

Clause 7 is a residuary clause wherein you can give the remainder of your estate. This provision is important in case you have omitted to give any of your property under clause 6, or if any of your other gifts should fail for any reason.

You should date and sign your will with your legal signature in the presence of your witnesses.

Other Clauses for Your Will

Depending on your particular circumstances you may want to include additional provisions in your will, such as a guardianship clause and trust clause for your minor children, a simultaneous death clause, or predeceased clause in case a beneficiary should predecease you. These sample clauses are given at the end of this chapter and can be included in clause 8 of the sample will.

The guardianship clause nominates someone whom you would like to act as guardian of your minor children. The trust clause provides the terms and conditions as to how a gift to your minor children will be held and distributed. In the trust clause, you should appoint a trustee and give instructions as to how the trustee should distribute the gifts. The simultaneous death clause provides that, if you and a beneficiary should die together, the gift to that beneficiary will pass through your estate rather than the estate of the beneficiary. The predeceased clause provides that, if beneficiaries should die before you, their gifts will pass to their lawful descendents who survive you. Otherwise the gifts become part of your residuary estate. You may also want to include a pledge of your body or organs in your will. A discussion on how to make such a pledge is provided in Chapter 7.

Revoking Your Will

You can revoke your will at any time before your death. You can revoke your will by tearing, cancelling, burning, or otherwise destroying it with the intent of revoking it. Your will can also be revoked by making a new will. Your new will can revoke the old one by explicit language of revocation or by conflicting provisions. The best ways of revoking a will are to execute a new will which expressly revokes the old one, or to cancel or otherwise revoke the will in the presence of witnesses.

Checklist for Preparing Your Will

❏ Prepare a list of all real estate and personal property.

❏ Prepare a list of children, family members, and other beneficiaries.

❏ Prepare a plan of distribution of your property.

❏ Identify an Executor or Executrix for your estate.

❏ Prepare your will according to your wishes using the sample will form.

❏ Obtain three witnesses who will not be beneficiaries under your will.

❏ Sign and date your will in the presence of the witnesses.

❏ Have the witnesses sign your will in your presence and in the presence of each other.

❏ For a "self-proving" will, have the signatures notarized.

❏ Consult an attorney if your will involves complicated or difficult provisions.

Last Will and Testament

1. I, _____, being of sound mind and body and free will, and having full testamentary intent and capacity, do hereby voluntarily make, publish, and execute this document as my Last Will and Testament.

2. My current domicile is as follows: _____   _____
   _____

3. I hereby revoke all wills and codicils previously executed by me.

4. I hereby appoint _____ as Executor/Executrix of my estate. I direct that no bond be required in any jurisdiction for the faithful exercise of his/her duties.

5. I hereby direct my Executor/Executrix to pay all of my just debts and other expenses of the administration of my estate.

6. I hereby devise and give the following items:

7. All the rest, residue, and remainder of my estate, whether real or personal, I devise and give as follows:

8. Other provisions:

In Witness Whereof, I have signed this document as my Last Will and Testament on this _____ day of _____ 19__.

_____
Legal Signature

The foregoing Will of _____, dated _____, was signed and published in our presence as his/her Last Will and Testament. We declare that the maker was of sound mind and body and free will at that time, and we have hereto signed our names as witnesses in the presence of the maker and of each other.

_____   _____
Witness' Signature   Address

_____   _____
Witness' Signature   Address

_____   _____
Witness' Signature   Address

Subscribed and sworn to before me on this _____ day of _____, 19__.

_____
Notary

Sample Clauses for Wills

Guardianship Clause

I hereby nominate and appoint _____ as the Guardian of any of my children during their respective minority ages and upon my death.

Simultaneous Death Clause

If any beneficiary named in this Will and I shall die together, or under any circumstances where it is impracticable to determine the order of death, I hereby direct that the terms of this Will shall be construed as if said beneficiary had predeceased me and that my estate shall be administered accordingly.

Predeceased Clause

If any beneficiary named in this will shall predecease me, then I hereby direct that his/her bequest, devise, or gift shall be given by per stirpes right of representation to his/her lawful descendents who are living at the time of my death. If said beneficiary leaves no lawful descendents who are living at the time of my death, then his/her gift shall lapse and become part of my residuary estate.

Trust Clause for Minor Children

If any of my children named as a beneficiary under this Will is a minor at the time of my death, then I direct that his/her bequest, devise, or gift under this Will shall be held in trust by my Executor/Executor as Trustee, and distributed according to the following terms and conditions for the support, maintenance and education of said children:

Codicil

1. I, _____, being of sound mind and body and free will, and having full testamentary intent and capacity, do hereby voluntarily make, publish and execute this document as a codicil to my Last Will and Testament which was made on the _____ day of _____, 19___.

2. I hereby amend and modify the provisions of my Last Will and Testament identified above as follows:

3. Except as expressly modified by this codicil, all remaining terms and provisions of my Last Will and Testament identified above shall remain in full force and effect.

In Witness Whereof, I have signed this document as a codicil to my Last Will and Testament identified above on this _____ day of _____, 19___.

_____
Maker's Signature

The foregoing codicil of _____, dated this _____ day of_____, 19___, was signed and published in our presence as a codicil to his/her Last Will and Testament. We declare that the maker was of sound mind and body and free will at that time, and we have hereto signed our names as witnesses in the presence of the maker and of each other.

_____   _____
Witness' Signature   Address

_____   _____
Witness' Signature   Address

_____   _____
Witness' Signature   Address

Subscribed and sworn to before me on this _____ day of _____, 19___.

_____
Notary

4 *Easy Steps to Probate a Will*

Definition of Probate

Probate is the legal process by which your estate is settled and the property of your estate distributed. In general, this process involves settling all of your accounts and debts, paying any applicable estate and inheritance taxes, and distributing your property to your beneficiaries or heirs.

Probate proceedings are generally held in the probate court in the county and state where you resided on the date of your death. If you do not leave a will, your estate will be administered and distributed according to the law of inheritance of your state. If you have prepared a will, it will be offered for probate and your estate will be administered according to your will.

Your will has no real effect until it has been probated. The procedures for probate of a will vary for each state, but they generally require the filing of a petition or application for probate with the probate court. Your will can be offered for probate by anyone who has an interest in your estate. If no will is involved, a petition for the appointment of an administrator and administration of your estate would have to be filed.

Obviously, you will not be handling the probate of your own estate after your death. However, the information in this chapter will be useful to others who will be probating your estate, and to you if you should ever have to probate the estate of a deceased family member or friend.

Procedures for Probating an Estate

The procedures for probating an estate are governed by the law of the state where the decedent was domociled. If real estate is located in other states, supplementary probate proceedings may also be required in those states to setle title to any real estate.

Generally a sworn petition or application for probate is filed in the probate court of the county where the decedent had his or her last domicile. The petition or application may be filed by the Executor or Executrix, a beneficiary, an heir, a creditor, or anyone with a claim against or interest in the estate. The petition or application should include a copy of any will, the decedent's death certificate, and a list of decedent's surviving spouse, next of kin, and heirs at law known to the petitioner or applicant. A hearing is scheduled by the court to settle claims and approve the disposition of the estate assets. The petitioner/applicant is usually required to publish notice of the probate hearing in the newspaper and send notice to any person known to have an interest in the decedent's estate.

Using the Sample Petition/Application to Probate a Will

A sample petition/application to probate a will is provided at the end of this chapter. This petition/application can be completed and filed without the assistance of an attorney if the probate proceeding is a simple one. However, if you decide to hire an attorney in a complex probate, be certain to find an attorney who is experienced in handling estate and probate matters. Typical attorney's fees in probate cases range from about three percent to about seven percent of the value of your decedent's estate. The Executor, Executrix or other administrator is generally paid a fee for administering the estate in the range of three percent to five percent of the value of the estate. These legal and administrative fees are usually paid out of the proceeds of the decedent's estate. The time and expense of probate can be avoided by setting up a living trust. Information and forms for setting up a living trust are presented in Chapter 5.

The caption of the sample petition/application should include the full name of the decedent and the name of the court. The docket number is obtained from the court clerk at the time the petition/application is filed. Be sure to check with the court clerk to find out if multiple copies of the petition/application must be filed and what filing fees may be involved. You should keep one copy of the petition/ application for your records.

Item 1 of the sample petition/application should include the complete address of the petitioner/applicant.

Item 2 should include the date and place of death of the decedent.

The decedent's domicile at the time of his or her death should be included in item 3. Remember that the decedent's domicile is important in determining the place of probate. A person's domicile is his or her fixed or permanent place of residence.

Item 4 makes reference to a list of decedent's surviving spouse, heirs at law, and next of kin which are known to you, the petitioner/applicant. This list should be attached to the petition/application as an exhibit.

Item 5 makes reference to the decedent's Last Will and Testament. A copy of the decedent's will should be attached to the petition/application as an exhibit.

Reference is made to the decedent's Death Certificate in item 6. A copy of the decedent's Death Certificate should be attached to the petition/application as an exhibit.

Item 7 is a certification that all information in the petition/application is true.

You should sign the petition/application and include your address and telephone number for easy reference by the probate court. Because some courts may require that your signature be verified, (particularly if someone else will be filing the petition/application on your behalf) it should be notarized.

The sample petition/application is adaptable for use in most states for probating an estate where a valid will is involved. You should check the rules and requirements for your particular state. If no will is involved, the petition/application should be one for administration of the decedent's estate. In such a case, item 4 of the sample petition/application is deleted and replaced with a declaration that the decedent has not left a will. The application should also contain a clause, such as the following: Petitioner/Applicant requests that _____ be appointed as administrator of the decedent's estate.

Checklist for Filing Petition/ Application for Probate

❏ Obtain a copy of decedent's Last Will and Testament

❏ Obtain a copy of decedent's Death Certificate.

❏ Prepare a list of decedent's surviving spouse, heirs at law, and next of kin. Also prepare a list of creditors of the decedent's estate if this is required by the probate court.

❏ Complete Petition/Application to Probate Will. Attach a copy of decedent's Last Will and Testament and a list of decedent's spouse, heirs, and next of kin.

❏ Sign and date the petition/application and have it notarized if required by the probate court.

❏ File the petition with the appropriate probate court.

❏ If the decedent did not leave a will, prepare and file a petition/application for administration of decedent's estate and appointment of an administrator.

❏ Consult an attorney if the probate of decedent's estate will involve complex or difficult issues.

Petition/Application to Probate Will

Estate of _____ , Deceased.   *Court: _____

*Docket No.: _____

Petitioner/Applicant, _____ (Name of petitioner/applicant),
declares the following:

1. Petitioner/Applicant resides at _____

_____ .

2. Decedent died on _____(Date) at_____(Place of Death).

3. Decedent's domicile at the time of his/her death was_____

_____ .

4. Attached is a list of decedent's surviving spouse, heirs at law, and next of kin known to the petitioner/applicant.

5. Attached is decedent's Last Will and Testament executed on _____(Date).

6. Attached is a copy of the Death Certificate of _____(Name of Decedent).

7. Petitioner/Applicant certifies that all information contained herein is true to the best of his/her knowledge and belief.

_____   _____
Signature   Date

_____
Address

_____
Phone

Subscribed and sworn to before me this _____ day of_____, 19_____.

_____
Notary

5 *Using a Living Trust to Avoid Probate*

Making Use of a Living Trust

A living or "inter vivos" trust can be used to avoid the expenses, time, and procedures of probating your estate. Basically, a living trust is the establishment of a separate legal entity during your lifetime to hold, manage, and distribute property according to the terms of a trust agreement.

A living trust can serve important functions in planning your estate for both probate and tax purposes. If you retain the right to revoke the trust, your estate must pay federal estate taxes on the trust assets. Also, income that the revocable trust earns will be taxable to you even if this income is paid to someone else. Federal estate taxes can be avoided by making the trust irrevocable or revocable only upon the occurrence of an event outside of your control.

A trust is established when you transfer real estate or personal property to someone to act as trustee pursuant to a trust agreement. A valid trust requires that title to the trust property actually be transferred to the trust. This is generally done by transferring the property to the trustee with a designation such as "to Carl Battle, trustee." The requirements as to who can serve as a trustee are governed by the laws of your specific state. Generally, any person or entity which is capable of contracting can serve as trustee. The trustee usually is a bank, an insurance company, a certified public accountant, an attorney, or any other person competent in business affairs. In many states, you can be the maker (or "settlor") of the trust and also serve as trustee, provided that you are not the only beneficiary.

Assets that you transfer to a living trust are generally not included in your estate for probate purposes. Instead, the assets of your living trust are distributed by your trustee according to the terms of your trust agreement. Therefore, it is important that your trust agreement provide for the disposition of trust property and income after your death, particularly if you are the trustee or the initial life beneficiary. If you are the trustee, it is also important that you have appointed an alternate trustee in case of your death so that the trust provisions can be carried out.

Any property can be transferred to your living trust, whether it is real or personal property. The trust agreement can also provide for additional property to be added to the trust in the future. Your living trust can also be coordinated with your will to avoid probate by providing that any property that would be probated shall be transferred to your living trust upon your death. The trust property should be handled separately from and not commingled with your individual property or the trust may be invalidated as merely a sham.

There are many tax and estate issues that may arise in setting up a trust. Complicated and difficult trust arrangement may require the assistance of an attorney or tax specialist. Typical legal fees for establishing a simple trust range from about $300 to $1000.

Understanding the Trust Agreement

A sample trust agreement is provided at the end of this chapter. The sample trust agreement is designed to be simple and adaptable for use in most situations. Each trust is a unique arrangement which should be tailored to your desires. Therefore, it is important that you complete the provisions of the trust agreement with clear terms and conditions that reflect your particular wishes.

The trust agreement is made between you (the maker or "settlor") and the trustee. Remember, you can serve as settlor and trustee in many states.

In Item 1(a) of the sample trust agreement you identify the property that you are transferring to the trust. You may make future transfers of property, but these should be clearly identified as transfers of property to the trust pursuant to your trust agreement.

Item 2 provides that you may revoke or amend the trust agreement except as provided by any terms and conditions that you may specify.

Item 3 provides for the payment of the trust income during your lifetime to any beneficiary and according to any terms you indicate.

In Item 4 you can specify the beneficiaries and terms for the distribution of trust income and trust property upon your death.

Item 5 is a spendthrift provision which may protect the trust income and property from the legal claims of creditors of the beneficiaries. The spendthrift provision may not be effective if the settlor is the sole beneficiary. Item 6 gives the trustee broad powers to manage the trust in the trustee's best judgment and discretion. Item 7 appoints an alternate trustee in the event of the death, resignation, or incapacity of the initial trustee.

Item 8 provides for the trustee to receive reasonable compensation or be paid as otherwise agreed. The trustee is also reim-

bursed for trust expenses and not required to post a bond. Item 9 provides that any pertinent taxes on trust property shall be paid from the trust.

To avoid the "rule against perpetuities," item 10 provides that the trust shall not continue for more than 21 years after the later of your death or the death of the last surviving beneficiary. Any trust property remaining thereafter will be distributed according to the terms that you specify.

In item 11 you identify the state where the trust agreement is made and will be interpreted and administered.

The trust agreement should be signed by both the settlor and trustee. If you will be serving as the trustee of your trust, then you should sign the trust agreement both as the settlor and trustee.

**Checklist for
Establishing a Living Trust**

❑ Prepare a list of property which you will transfer to the trust.

❑ Prepare a list of beneficiaries and your plan for the distribution of trust income and trust property.

❑ Identify a trustee and an alternate.

❑ Prepare the trust agreement according to your plan of distribution and wishes.

❑ Settlor and Trustee sign the trust agreement.

❑ Transfer any identified property to the trust.

❑ If your trust involves difficult tax or estate issues, consult an attorney.

Trust Agreement

It is declared that, this Trust Agreement has been made and executed on this _____ day of _____, 19____,
between _____(the "Settlor")
_____(address)
and _____(the "Trustee")
_____(address)
according to the following terms and conditions:

1. **(a)** The property listed below is transferred by the Settlor to the Trustee, and the Trustee's successor in trust, subject to the terms, conditions, and purposes set forth herein:

   b) The property listed above and any other property that the Trustee may acquire pursuant to this Agreement (hereinafter "Trust Property"), shall be held, administered and distributed by the Trustee in accordance with the provisions of this Trust Agreement.

2. The Settlor may revoke or amend this Trust Agreement in writing at any time during his/her lifetime; except as provided by the following terms and conditions:

3. The Trustee shall pay and distribute the net income from this trust during the lifetime of the Settlor to the following beneficiary or beneficiaries and pursuant to the following terms:

4. Upon the death of the Settlor, the Trustee shall pay and distribute the net income from this trust and the Trust Property to the following beneficiary or beneficiaries and pursuant to the following terms:

5. The interests of the beneficiaries in the Trust Property and trust income shall not be subject to the claims of their creditors or any other party by way of garnishment, attachment, or any other legal process, and shall not be transferred or encumbered. Any such transfer or encumberance shall be null and void.

6. The Trustee shall have the power pursuant to this Trust Agreement to hold, manage, operate, lease, sell, exchange, convey, repair, insure, protect, and invest the Trust Property and to collect the trust income and to employ other's assistance, all in the Trustee's best judgment and discretion.

7. In the event of death, resignation or other incapacity of the Trustee first named herein, the following person, persons or entity shall serve as the Trustee pursuant to this Trust Agreement:

8. The Trustee shall be entitled to receive reasonable and just compensation, or be paid as otherwise provided by agreement, for the Trustee's services, and shall be reimbursed for all reasonable expenses incurred in managing the Trust Property. The Trustee shall not be required to post a bond in any state for the exercise of the Trustee's duties pursuant to this Trust Agreement.

9. If any estate, inheritance, or transfer taxes are assessed against the Trust Property, the Trustee shall pay such taxes from the Trust Property.

10. No trust established herein shall continue for more than 21 years after the death of the last survivor of the Settlor or any beneficiary named herein. At the expiration of such period any Trust property remaining shall be immediately distributed as follows:

11. This Trust Agreement has been made in and shall be interpreted and administered in accordance with the laws of the State of _____.

Settlor and Trustee, intending to be legally bound, have signed this Agreement on the date first indicated above.

_____
Settlor's Signature

_____
Trustee's Signature

Subscribed and sworn to before me on this _____ day of _____, 19___.

_____
Notary

6 Making a Living Will

The Functions of a Living Will

A "living will" is not a will at all, but instructions and a power of attorney to family members or doctors regarding the continuation or termination of medical life-support systems. Living Wills can be useful to avoid life-support systems which only prolong the dying process.

Beginning with California in 1976, 37 other states and the District of Columbia adopted "living will," "death-with-dignity," or "right-to-die" laws which recognize the rights of terminally ill patients to stop life-support. At the time of this printing, the other states which recognize living wills are Alabama, Alaska, Arizona, Arkansas, Colorado, Connecticut, Delaware, Florida, Georgia, Hawaii, Idaho, Illinois, Indiana, Iowa, Kansas, Louisiana, Maine, Maryland, Mississippi, Missouri, Montana, Nevada, New Hampshire, New Mexico, North Carolina, Oklahoma, Oregon, South Carolina, Tennessee, Texas, Utah, Vermont, Virginia, Washington, West Virginia, Wisconsin, and Wyoming. The purpose of these laws is to protect doctors, hospitals, and others from civil and criminal liability and to honor the wishes of patients who are dying from a terminal condition.

The requirements for making a living will vary for each state. Generally, the laws require that the living will be signed and dated by the maker. It generally must be witnessed by two or more people who are not the maker's relatives, doctor (or doctor's employees), beneficiaries, or creditors. The maker and witnesses generally must be of legal age (i.e., 18 years old in most states). If you make a living will, give copies to your doctor and family so that they will know your wishes.

A typical "death with dignity" law provides that a terminally ill patient can request by a conscious directive or by a living will that life-support systems be withheld or withdrawn. The hospital, staff, and family will be free from liability if such a request is honored. The laws also protect any insurance that the terminal patient may have, by declaring that honoring a living will does not constitute suicide.

The living will document itself basically provides: If the situation should arise in which there is no reasonable expectation of recovery from terminal physical or mental disability, you request that you be allowed to die naturally, and not be kept alive by artificial means or extraordinary measures.

Before your living will is honored, usually a determination of terminal illness must be made by your attending physician and at least one other doctor. However, the living will must normally be made by you when you are in a stable mental and physical condition. You can revoke or modify your living will at any time.

Some doctors or hospitals may be reluctant to honor a living will and terminate life support systems. For this reason, many states allow you to make a durable power of attorney or medical proxy whereby you appoint someone to make medical decisions for you when you are unable to do so. The medical proxies and durable power of attorney are more likely to be honored by doctors and hospitals, because someone has been appointed by you who can make decisions regarding specific circumstances as they arise.

The following jurisdictions recognize medical proxies or durable powers of attorney whereby you can appoint someone to make medical decisions, including withdrawal or withholding of life support: Arizona, California, Colorado, Florida, Georgia, Hawaii, Iowa, Illinois, Kansas, Kentucky, Maine, Maryland, Massachusetts, Michigan, Mississippi, Nevada, New Jersey, New York, Ohio, Oregon, Rhode Island, South Carolina, South Dakota, Tennessee, Texas, Vermont, Virginia, West Virginia, Wisconsin, and the District of Columbia.

It is recommended that a medical proxy or durable power of attorney be included in your living will. A sample living will form is provided at the end of this chapter and is adaptable for use in most jurisdictions. It incorporates a durable power of attorney.

Checklist for Making a Living Will

❑ Check to see if your state recognizes living wills and what the requirements are.

❑ Identify two or more people as witnesses who are not your family members, doctors, beneficiaries, or creditors.

❑ Identify someone that you can appoint to make medical decisions if you are incapacitated.

❑ Prepare and sign your living will. Also have your witnesses sign your living will. It is recommended that your living will be notarized.

❑ Give copies of your living will to your appointed agent, your family, and your doctor.

❑ If your living will involves difficult or complex issues, you should consult an attorney.

Living Will

1. I, _____(Maker), being of sound mind voluntarily declare that this directive is made this _____ day of _____, 19_____ as my Living Will in accordance with the laws of the State of _____.

2. If I should have at any time an incurable condition caused by illness, disease, or injury certified to be a terminal condition by two licensed physicians, and where there is no reasonable expectation of recovery from said terminal condition, and where the application of life-sustaining methods and equipment would only prolong the moment of my imminent death, I hereby direct and request that said life-sustaining methods and equipment not be used, and that I be allowed to die naturally and not be kept alive by artificial or extraordinary means.

3. In the event that I am unable to give conscious direction regarding medical treatment or the use of said life-sustaining procedures, I direct and request that this Living Will be honored by my family, physicians and all others as the final and conclusive expression of my legal right to refuse medical treatment. I hereby appoint _____ as my true and lawful attorney in fact to act for me and make decisions concerning medical treatment, including the withdrawal or withholding of life support, in accordance with this Living Will. This power of attorney shall remain in effect in the event that I should become or be declared disabled, incapacitated, or incompetent.

4. This Living Will shall be in effect until it is revoked by me.

5. My current residence is: _____

In Witness Whercof I have signed this document as my declaration and Living Will.

_____   _____
Maker's signature   Date

The maker of this Living Will is personally known to me, is of sound mind, and has executed this document of his or her own free will.

_____   _____
Witness' Signature   Address

_____   _____
Witness' Signature   Address

_____   _____
Witness' Signature   Address

Subscribed and sworn to before me on this _____ day of _____, 19__.

_____
Notary

7 How to Make an Organ Donor Pledge

Making a Gift of Your Body or Organ

Upon your death, you may wish to donate certain of your organs or body parts for medical or other purposes. Every state and the District of Columbia have enacted laws permitting and regulating gifts of your human body, organs or parts thereof. These gifts can be made by your last will and testament or by any other document which gives or pledges your body or body parts.

Normally, it is the right and obligation of your spouse, children, parents, other family members, or guardian to dispose of your body after your death. However, you can direct what happens to your body in your will or pledge. These pledges can be extremely useful for medical therapy, transplantation, education, and research.

The laws governing gifts of the human body or body parts are similar in all the states. The laws generally provide that any person of sound mind and 18 years of age or more may give all or any part of his or her body for any permitted purpose. These gifts can generally be made to any hospital, doctor, medical school, university, or storage facility for the purposes of medical or dental education, research, therapy, or transplantation. The gifts can also be made to any individual for therapy or transplantation needed by him or her.

If you make a gift or pledge of your body or body parts without identifying a donee or recipient, your attending physician usually may accept the gift as donee. Your attending physician can then donate your body or parts according to his or her best judgement.

Your pledge of your body or organs supersedes the desires of your spouse, family, and others as to the disposition of your body. If you make a pledge, you should review it with your family and doctor to make your wishes known.

Your gift of your body or organs, whether by your will or other documents, takes effect only upon your death.

You can make your pledge at any time. You can make a pledge of your body, organs or parts by including an appropriate donor clause in your will. A sample donor clause for your will is included at the end of this chapter. A discussion on how to prepare your will can be found in chapter 3.

You can also make a gift or pledge by a written document other than your will. This document spells out the nature of your gift, the donee, and the purpose of your gift. The document must be signed by you, generally in the presence of two or more witnesses. The pledge document can be prepared in the form of a card which is carried on you. Many states allow a pledge to be printed on the back of your driving license. A sample pledge form is provided on the next page.

Pledge of Human Body, Organ or Part Thereof

1. I, _____ (Donor's name),

residing at _____ (Donor's address)

am of sound mind and 18 years or more of age.

2. Effective upon my death, I hereby pledge and give to _____ (Donee's name)

_____ (Donee's address)

my body or parts thereof as indicated and marked below:

      ❑   my entire body.

      ❑   any needed body part or organ.

      ❑   the following named organ(s) or body part(s):_____

_____

If the Donee named above is unable to accept or receive the above pledge, said pledge shall be given to the attending physician at my death.

3. My gift above shall be used only for the purpose(s) indicated and marked below:

      ❑   for transplant

      ❑   for therapy

      ❑   for medical research

      ❑   for medical education

      ❑   any lawful purposes

In Witness Whereof I have signed my name in the presence of the witnesses below.

_____   _____
Donor's Signature   Date

_____   _____
Witness' Signature   Address

_____   _____
Witness' Signature   Address

_____   _____
Witness' Signature   Address

8

Transferring Your Personal Rights by an Assignment

What Is an Assignment?

An assignment is a transfer of property, or any rights or interests therein, from one person to another. Usually assignments are used to transfer title to personal property as well as contractual rights, rights to payment, rights to sue, and other rights connected with both personal property and real estate.

The person transferring or assigning rights is referred to as the assignor. The assignee is the person to whom rights are transferred.

What Rights Are Assignable?

Generally all of your rights are assignable to another unless there is an agreement to the contrary or the assignment is against public policy and prohibited by law.

You can assign your right to receive payment or other benefits under a contract. This can include rights such as the rights to rental payments under a lease, payments under a promissory note, compensation under an employment agreement, royalties, dividends, and many others. Unlike your right to payment, your obligations to perform under a contract generally are not assignable, particularly if the contract is one for your personal services.

You can also assign most rights in your personal property and real estate. However, title to real estate is generally transferred by a deed rather than an assignment. Title to your personal property, such as stocks, bonds, household furnishings, equipment, and the like can be transferred by an assignment. An assignment can be evidence of the transfer of title to your automobile, but it is normally required that you transfer the Certificate of Title.

Requirements for Making a Valid Assignment

An assignment is essentially a contract. Therefore, to make a valid assignment, you generally must be of legal age and have the legal mental capacity to enter into contracts. A valid assignment must be entered into voluntarily and be free of fraud, coercion, or duress. Also, for an assignment to be enforceable, it is usually required that both the assignor and assignee give consideration or something of value under the assignment. You can make a valid assignment as a gift to the assignee. However, the assignee generally cannot enforce the assignment against you unless he or she has paid or promised you something in return. Your assignment should be in writing.

When you make an assignment, your assignee generally cannot obtain any rights or interests in the assigned property which are greater than those you may have. This simply means that you cannot transfer anything more than what you have. The assigned property, in the hands of your assignee, is still subject to all claims, liens, or other interests which existed against the property before you assigned it.

You do not avoid any liability or obligation you may have regarding a contract or other property merely because you have assigned your rights and interests therein. For example, if you finance the purchase of a car, you do not avoid your obligations to pay back your loan by assigning the car to someone else. Likewise, when you sublet an apartment, you are still obligated to pay the rent to your landlord. You are released from any liabilities and obligations in an assignment only if the assignee and all other parties involved agree or consent to your release.

Using the Sample Assignment Form

A sample assignment form is provided at the end of this chapter. The sample assignment form should be adaptable for use in all the states.

Item 1 of the assignment should identify the assignor and assignor's address. It should also clearly identify the assignee and assignee's address. This clause provides for the assignment and transfer of all of your rights, title and interests to the assigned property or other interests. The assigned property, rights, and interests should be specifically and clearly identified in the assignment.

In item 2 you should include any terms and conditions which affect or govern the assignment. For example, this could include provisions for payments, inspections, releases, consents, and the like.

Item 3 includes the effective date of the assignment. Item 4 should specify which state laws the assignment shall be governed by.

The assignment should be signed and dated by the assignor and assignee. It should also be signed by other parties who are affected by the assignment to show their consent and acceptance.

It is recommended that the assignment be notarized.

Assignment

1. For valuable and sufficient consideration, _____(Assignor's name)
_____(Assignor's address),

hereby assigns and transfers to

_____(Assignee's name)
_____(Assignee's address),

all of his/her rights, title, and interest in and to the following:

2. This assignment is subject to the following terms and conditions:

3. This assignment is effective on the _____ day of _____, 19__.

4. This assignment shall be governed by the laws of the State of _____.

In Witness Whereof, I have signed this Assignment of my own free will.

_____   _____
Assignor's Signature   Date

Agreed to and Accepted by:

_____   _____
Assignee's Signature   Date

Other Parties: _____   _____
                              Signature   Date

Subscribed and sworn to before me this _____ day of_____, 19___.

_____
Notary

9

Operating Through Someone Else by Power of Attorney

Understanding the Power of Attorney

A power of attorney is basically a written document which authorizes someone else to act on behalf of and as agent for you. If you make a power of attorney, you are commonly referred to as the *principal*. The person to whom you have given the power of attorney to act on your behalf is referred to as the *attorney in fact* or *agent*.

Your power of attorney can be a general power of attorney which authorizes your agent to conduct your entire business and affairs. A limited or special power of attorney authorizes your agent to conduct specified business or perform a single act on your behalf.

Your power of attorney primarily serves as evidence to others of your principal-agent relationship created by your power of attorney. It also serves as an agreement between you and your agent regarding the business to be transacted under your power of attorney.

A power of attorney can be useful in a variety of situations. For example, a power of attorney could be useful when you do not have the legal capacity or the time to manage your affairs. It can also be useful if you are incapacitated, undergoing an operation, or going away for a while. You may give a power of attorney to a real estate agent to manage, lease, or sell your home or apartment.

For almost anything that you can do for yourself, you can give a power of attorney to someone to act on your behalf. This includes the power to contract, buy and sell property, sign checks, make deposits and withdrawals, settle claims, file lawsuits, and almost anything else.

By their very nature, powers of attorney are serious documents which should be given careful consideration. Particularly with the broad general power of attorney, you should make certain your agent is trustworthy and competent.

Requirements for Making A Power of Attorney

Powers of attorney are usually governed by the laws regulating agents for the state where the power of attorney is made or the acts will be performed. Generally, any person who has the legal capacity to contract or appoint an agent can give his or her power of attorney to another person, corporation or other entities. The principal should be of legal age and mentally competent.

You can make a *durable power of attorney* which will remain valid even if you later lose the capacity to contract and appoint an agent. Your durable power of attorney must be in writing and must contain language which shows that you intend the power of attorney to remain in effect even if you are disabled or incapacitated.

Any power of attorney that you make should be in writing. It should include your name and address as the principal. It should also include the name and address of your agent. You should indicate the status of your agent as an individual, corporation, association, etc.

Your power of attorney should clearly show the scope and extent of the powers granted. It should indicate whether the power of attorney is a *general* or a *limited* one. It should include the effective date and the time period during which the power of attorney will be in effect. To the extent possible, you should list the specific acts which are to be performed by your agent.

Property which is subject to your power of attorney should be clearly described. Indicate the nature, ownership and location of such property, whether personal property, securities, real estate, and the like.

It is recommended that a provision be included which covers the manner by which you can revoke your power of attorney. Remember that if you want your power of attorney to be a durable one you must include a provision that it shall remain in effect if you become incapacitated.

If you intend for your agent to be compensated for the agent's services, indicate the amount and manner of compensation.

Your power of attorney should be signed and dated by both you as the principal and by your agent. It is recommended that your power of attorney be notarized. Some states require that powers of attorney dealing with the sale or conveyance of real estate be recorded in the county where the property is located. Be sure to check with your county clerk or recorder of deeds for specific requirements.

A sample durable power of attorney form is provided at the end of this chapter and will be useful for most situations. You can have an attorney draft a power of attorney for you at a cost ranging from about $100 to $300 depending on complexity and location.

Power of Attorney

1. I, _____(Principal's name)
_____(Principal's address),
being of sound mind and legal capacity, do hereby appoint _____(Agent's name)
_____(Agent's address),
as my true and lawful attorney in fact, to act for me in my name, place, and stead, and on my behalf to do and perform the following:

2. The following property, interests, or rights shall be subject to this Power of Attorney:

3. This Power of Attorney shall be effective on the date of _____,19___.

4. This Power of Attorney shall remain in effect in the event that I should become or be declared disabled, incapacitated, or incompetent.

5. This Power of Attorney shall terminate on the date of _____,19_____, unless I have revoked it sooner. I may revoke this Power of Attorney at any time and in any manner.

6. My agent shall be paid compensation for services pursuant to this Power of Attorney as follows:

7. This Power of Attorney shall be governed by the laws of the State of _____.

In Witness Whereof, I have signed this Power of Attorney of my own free will.

_____   _____
Principal's Signature   Date

Agreed to and Accepted by:

_____   _____
Agent's Signature   Date

Subscribed and sworn to before me on this _____ day of_____,19____.

_____
Notary

Chapter

10 *Buying and Selling Your Home*

Understanding Real Estate Sales

The purchase of a home or other real estate is probably the largest single expenditure you will make during your lifetime. The average home can cost between $100,000 and $200,000 (depending upon location) and, when your principal and interest payments are combined, your total costs can exceed three or four times the purchase price.

The purchase and sale of real estate such as land, a house, an apartment, or a condominium can involve many issues such as ownership, type of deed, fire and title insurance, liens, mortgage contingencies, taxes, and more. If you are buying or selling real estate of any size or magnitude, you need to be as informed as possible about the legal and financial matters involved.

It is customary for both the seller and the buyer to obtain an attorney to represent each in the transaction. The attorney can usually handle the preparation of the agreement of sale, deed, and other documents, and assist in arrangements for the title search and financing. Typical attorney fees for simple real estate transactions vary with location, but usually range from approximately $500 to $1,000.

If you are knowledgeable in real estate transactions, you may be able to save legal expenses by handling some or all of these activities yourself. You may also obtain help from your real estate broker, mortgage lender, or title insurance company.

Using a Real Estate Agent

Most real estate sales are made through a licensed real estate agent (or broker) with whom the seller has listed the property. The real estate broker is basically an agent for the seller and acts as an intermediary between buyer and seller in procuring the sale. Generally, the broker acts based upon a written listing agreement with the seller and will receive a commission if a successful sale is completed.

If you are the buyer, any services the real estate agent gives you are usually free of charge. Be aware that the agent represents the interests of the seller and not the buyer. However, if you are selling property, you typically pay a commission to your agent which can range from about five percent to seven percent of the sales price.

When you list your property with a real estate agent, you can enter into an exclusive or a nonexclusive listing. With an exclusive listing, the agent will receive his or her commission if the property is sold, even if you or someone else obtains the buyer. If the listing is nonexclusive, the broker receives a commission only if he or she actually finds the buyer. Although an exclusive listing locks you in with the agent for the term of the listing agreement, the agent is normally under a duty to use good faith efforts to find a buyer who is ready, willing, and able.

A sample listing agreement is provided at the end of this chapter. The listing agreement should include the names and addresses of the owner and the agent. It should have an address, location, and written description of the real estate property being listed for sale. Make sure the listing agreement indicates whether it is an exclusive or a non-exclusive listing. Include the agent's compensation as a percentage of the gross sales price paid to or retained as deposits by the owner. Other important provisions for you to consider are a minimum sales price, listing of any personal property to be included, a termination date, and a designation of the governing state law. Make sure that the term of the listing agreement is not too long. A term of 3 to 6 months is usually sufficient. The listing agreement is signed by both the owner and the agent. It is recommended that the listing agreement be notarized.

Making a Real Estate Agreement of Sale

The sale of real estate property ordinarily begins with the buyer and seller entering into a contract or agreement of sale. Next to the deed, the agreement of sale is perhaps the most important document covering the real estate transaction.

The agreement of sale normally must be in writing and should include the names and addresses of the buyer and seller, the sales price and manner of payment, an adequate description of the property, the extent of title to be conveyed, the date of closing, and any other important terms and conditions. The agreement of sale is a negotiated document between the buyer and seller and should be fully understood and agreed to by both. If you are the purchaser, you should consider including clauses covering inspection for termites and other physical damage, fire and building code violations, and the buyer being able to obtain an acceptable mortgage.

The terms of the agreement of sale are very important to determine its validity and to support remedies for damages or specific performance in case of breach. Usually, the

seller's promise to convey the property and the buyer's promise to purchase for a certain price constitute valid consideration under the laws of contract. The description of the property must be sufficient to permit reference to specific property without ambiguity. It is recommended that the agreement of sale include a legal description from the prior deed as well as a street address and location. Any personal property which is included in the sale should be specifically identified in the agreement of sale.

The agreement of sale should clearly include the amount of the purchase price and the manner of payment, such as by cash, certified check, or electronic transfer. Often, the buyer will need to borrow money to pay for the property and should make the agreement of sale contingent upon the buyer obtaining an acceptable mortgage or financing. The mortgage contingency clause should specify the minimum amount of mortgage money required, the maximum acceptable interest rate, and the term of the mortgage (usually 30 years). The mortgage contingency clause should include a time period within which the buyer is required to obtain a mortgage commitment from a lending institution. The buyer is obligated to use reasonable and good faith efforts to obtain an acceptable mortgage.

The real estate agreement of sale should specify the type of title which will be conveyed to the buyer and the type of deed to be delivered (i.e. warranty deed or quitclaim deed). The agreement of sale generally implies that the seller will convey to the buyer a marketable title free of encumbrances. Such title gives the buyer an unrestricted right to transfer or dispose of the property. Marketable title is normally one which has reasonable validity, certainty, and freedom from attack in court.

The agreement of sale should state the date, time, and place of closing. If it is essential for closing to take place on the stated closing date, then the agreement of sale should indicate that time is of the essence. Both the buyer and seller should be ready, willing, and able to conclude the sale at closing. If time is made of the essence for closing, any party who is not ready and able to close will be in breach of the agreement.

Sometimes, the agreement of sale is prepared from a pre-printed form by the real estate agent. It usually starts as a signed offer from the buyer which is later accepted and signed by the seller. Both buyer and seller should feel free to consult an attorney and to modify the agreement of sale before signing by adding or deleting provisions in the agreement. The agreement of sale must be signed by both buyer and seller or their authorized representatives for the agreement to be legally enforceable.

It is customary for the buyer to pay a deposit (typically one percent to five percent of the purchase price) upon signing the agreement of sale. This deposit is usually applied toward the purchase price. However, the disposition of the deposit should be clearly spelled out in the agreement of sale. The agreement of sale may provide that any deposit will be forfeited to the seller as liquidated damages if the buyer breaches the agreement. It is recommended that the deposit be held in escrow with instructions as to its disposition should either the buyer or seller breach the agreement of sale.

After the real estate agreement of sale has been signed by both parties, the buyer normally becomes the equitable owner of the property. Unless the agreement of sale provides otherwise, the buyer assumes the risk of damages or destruction of the property after the agreement has been fully signed. The buyer is well advised to purchase insurance to protect his or her interest or to include a provision in the agreement of sale that the risks of loss or damage remain with the seller until closing. Likewise, it is recommended that the seller maintain insurance in force if the agreement of sale provides for the seller to assume the risk of loss.

A sample Real Estate Agreement of Sale is provided at the end of this chapter and is adaptable for use in most states.

Obtaining Financing for Your Real Estate Purchase

There are a number of financing arrangements and sources available to you for the purchase of real estate. Financing for the purchase of residential property is usually cheaper and easier to obtain than financing for commercial and investment properties. For example, if you are purchasing a house or other residential property, you may be able to obtain conventional, Federal National Mortgage Association (FNMA), Federal Housing Administration (FHA), Veteran's Administration (VA), purchase money mortgage, mortgage assumption, or land contract financing.

Conventional financing normally involves the borrowing of money from a regular lending institution, where the loan is not guaranteed by a third party. On the other hand, depending on your qualifications, you may be able to obtain an insured mortgage loan, such as FNMA, FHA or VA, whereby a governmental agency or private mortgage company guarantees or insures repayment of the loan if you should default. The insured financing can usually be obtained with a relatively low down payment (i.e., ten percent or less) while conventional financing may require as much as a twenty percent to thirty percent down payment.

Other financing options with a conventional mortgage are a fixed rate or an adjustable rate mortgage. A fixed rate mortgage has a constant interest rate over the entire term of the mortgage loan. The interest rate for an adjustable rate loan is normally adjusted up or down within certain limits and is usually based on the prime rate, consumer price index, or other common economic indicators. Conventional mortgages normally have a term of 25-30 years and provide for equal monthly installment payments for the term of the loan.

A purchase money mortgage is a type of private financing in which the seller provides the financing. The seller takes back a mortgage and promissory note for the balance of the purchase price in this situation.

A land contract is similar to the purchase money mortgage, except that the seller will generally retain title to the property until all the payments have been made under the land contract. You should seriously consider all of the various types of financing and decide on the financing arrangements which are most suitable for you.

Typically, you will apply to banks, savings and loan associations, credit unions and other mortgage companies to secure financing for your real estate purchase. The lending institution will usually require a copy of the agreement of sale and financial and employment information on you. A nonrefundable loan application fee, which may range up to several hundred dollars, is frequently required by the lender. Most lenders will also require that you pay a loan origination fee or points if your loan is approved, which can amount to one percent to three percent of the mortgage amount. If your loan application is approved, a mortgage commitment letter specifying the terms of the mortgage will be given to you by the lending institution.

At closing the lender will usually require you to sign a mortgage and security agreement and a promissory note. The promissory note is essentially a negotiable document whereby you promise to pay a certain sum of money at a definite time. Generally the promissory note will be in writing and signed by you as the maker. A sample Promissory Note is provided at the end of this chapter.

Once you, the buyer, have accepted the mortgage commitment, you or your attorney may order a title search, obtain title and fire insurance, and handle other activities leading to closing. You should request from the seller copies of the seller's deed, any title insurance policies, any surveys of the property, and any other information concerning the title to the property. This information from the seller should be sent to the title insurance company which will be conducting the title search. Title insurance is generally required by the lender for its benefit

as a condition for the mortgage, but is is recommended that the buyer also obtain a buyer's policy to protect the buyer's own interests.

The seller, in preparing for closing, will clear the property of any liens or other encumbrances which are required to be satisfied. Also, the seller will usually make any necessary repairs and otherwise put the property in condition for delivery of possession to the buyer at closing.

What Happens at Closing?

The "closing" (or "settlement") is a very important step in the sale and purchase of real estate. This is usually the point when the real estate transaction is finalized, with the buyer receiving the deed and possession of the property and the seller receiving the purchase money. At closing, the buyer, seller, attorneys, real estate agents, a representative from the lending institution, and a representative from the title insurance company meet to review and sign all the necessary documents and proceed with closing.

The Federal Real Estate Settlement Procedures Act (RESPA) requires that the person conducting the closing (typically the real estate agent, title company, or mortgage lender) provide a settlement statement to the buyer and seller. RESPA also requires that the lender give to the buyer-borrower a good faith estimate of the closing costs when the mortgage loan application is made. RESPA applies to real estate transactions involving first mortgage loans for homes having no more than four separate units and financed by a federally related mortgage loan. This includes most residential mortgages, such as those from federally insured banks and savings and loans associations, FNMA, FHA, or VA. RESPA generally does not apply to mortgage assumptions, land contracts, second mortgages, or purchase money mortgages.

The settlement statement given at closing lists all settlement costs to be paid by buyer and seller. This settlement statement can be used by the buyer to determine how much money the buyer will actually need to bring to closing. Normally, the buyer is required to make payment at closing by certified check. The settlement statement also lets the seller know what items are being charged against the seller, such as seller's attorney's fees, real estate commissions, transfer taxes, and payoff of any existing mortgages and liens. If the seller has not taken care of the appropriate liens, encumbrances, or repairs to the property, some of the purchase money should be placed in escrow to take care of these.

At closing, the seller will have prepared a deed to the property which will be given to the buyer. Typically, title is transferred to the buyer by a general warranty deed which carries full guarantees of title against any and all claims, or by special warranty deed which guarantees title only against any claims by, through, or under the seller/grantor or seller/grantor's heirs. A quitclaim deed, on the other hand, conveys only that interest which the seller has, if any. A quitclaim deed makes no guarantees of title and is typically used when property is transferred as a gift or for minimal consideration. Remember that the agreement of sale should specify the type of deed to be delivered to the buyer at closing.

The deed generally must include the names of all the sellers-grantors and buyers-grantees, a legal description of the property, the appropriate clause granting title to the grantees, the date, and the signatures of the grantors and witnesses. Samples of a General Warranty Deed, Special Warranty Deed, and a Quitclaim Deed are provided at the end of this chapter. After closing, the buyer should have the deed recorded with the County Recorder or other appropriate office.

Once closing has concluded, the buyer receives his or her deed, title insurance policy, and possession of the property, while the seller receives the purchase money after adjustments for charges to the seller. In addition, the lender receives its mortgage agreement and promissory note from the buyer and the mortgagee's title insurance

policy from the title company. The real estate agents and attorneys are usually also paid at closing. If buyer and seller have realized their expectations, and have properly acted to protect their interests, the real estate transaction should close smoothly.

Checklist for Sale or Purchase of Real Estate

❏ If Seller, list property with real estate broker. Execute appropriate Real Estate Listing Agreement.

❏ Buyer and Seller sign Agreement of Sale.

❏ Include mortgage contingency clause if buyer will be obtaining a mortgage loan to purchase the property.

❏ Specify in Agreement of Sale the type of title and deed to be conveyed to buyer.

❏ Include a closing date in Agreement of Sale. Indicate if time is of the essence.

❏ Identify in Agreement of Sale any personal property to be included.

❏ If buyer, apply for any necessary mortgage financing and obtain mortgage commitment.

❏ If buyer, obtain title search and title insurance.

❏ If buyer, obtain fire and hazard insurance.

❏ Pre-closing inspection and testing for termites and other damage.

❏ If seller, clear property of any required liens and charges and make any necessary repairs.

❏ If seller, prepare appropriate deed to be delivered to buyer at closing.

❑ If buyer, obtain certified check or other appropriate means for payment of balance of settlement charges at closing.

❑ Close on the real estate transaction. Buyer signs any necessary mortgage agreements and promissory notes. Buyer delivers balance of purchase price to seller or closing agent. Seller delivers deed and possession of property to buyer.

❑ Buyer records deed with County Recorder or other appropriate office.

❑ Consult an attorney if the real estate transaction involves complex or difficult issues.

Real Estate Listing Agreement

1. This Listing Agreement is made and is effective this _____ day of _____, 19_____ by and between
_____(Owner's name)
_____(Owner's address)
and _____(Agent's name)
_____(Agent's address).

2. Owner has the legal right to enter into this Listing Agreement and has legal title to the real property located at
_____ (street address)
_____(city)_____(county)_____(state);
said property being specifically described as follows:

3. Agent is a licensed real estate agent or broker in good standing under the laws of the State of _____ and is authorized by law to represent Owner as a real estate agent or broker.

4. Owner hereby grants to Agent the right to offer for sale said property described above in accordance with the terms of this Listing Agreement. This right to Agent shall be: (check one)

   ❏   (a) exclusive
   ❏   (b) nonexclusive.

5. Owner shall pay to Agent on or before the date set for closing in any binding agreement with owner for the purchase and sale of said property a commission in the amount of ____ percent (____%) of the gross sale price actually paid to or forfeited to owner by a buyer, subject to the following provisions:

   (a) if Agent has an exclusive right to offer for sale said property as indicated in Item 4(a) above, said commission shall be payable in accordance with Item 5 above to Agent if any buyer executes a binding agreement with Owner for the purchase and sale of said property during the term of this Listing Agreement; and

   (b) if Agent has a nonexclusive right to offer for sale said property as indicated in Item 4(b) above, said commission shall be payable in accordance with Item 5 above to Agent only if a buyer procured by Agent executes a binding agreement with Owner for the purchase and sale of said property during the term of this Listing Agreement.

6. Agent is an independent contractor under this Listing Agreement, and Agent shall be responsible for any brokerage fees, commissions, or other compensation to other agents and employees in procuring a sale of said property pursuant to this Listing Agreement. Owner shall not be liable for any brokerage fees, commissions or other compensation except as provided in Item 5 above.

7. Agent is given authority under this Listing Agreement only to solicit offers from prospective buyers of said property. Agent shall have no authority to accept any offers from prospective buyers or to otherwise make any binding agreements on behalf of Owner. Agent shall not list or advertise said property at a price of less than $_____. Agent shall not assign or delegate any of Agent's duties and performance under this Listing Agreement without Owner's prior written consent.

8. Owner may accept or reject any offer from any prospective buyer at Owner's sole discretion.

9. Only the personal property specifically listed below is included in the sale of the real property covered by this Listing Agreement:

10. This Listing Agreement represents the entire agreement and understanding of Owner and Agent in reference to the property covered herein. This Listing Agreement shall terminate on the _____ day of _____,19_____.

11. This Listing Agreement shall be governed by the laws of the State of _____.

12. Owner and Agent hereby agree to the following additional terms and conditions:

Owner and Agent, intending to be legally bound, have signed this Agreement on the date first indicated above.

_____   _____
           Owner's signature   Agent's signature

Subscribed and sworn to before me on this _____ day of _____, 19_____.

_____
                     Notary

Real Estate Agreement of Sale

1. This Agreement is made on this _____ day of _____, 19_____ by and between
   _____(Buyer's name)
   _____(Buyer's address)
   and _____(Seller's name)
   _____(Seller's address).

2. Buyer shall purchase and Seller shall sell and convey to Buyer the property located at:
   _____(address of property),
   including the land and any and all buildings, structures, fixtures, improvements, easements, rights and privileges apper-
   taining thereto; said property being legally described as follows:

3. Only the personal property specifically listed below is included in the sale of the property covered by this Agreement:

4. Buyer shall pay to Seller a total purchase price for the Property in the amount of _____
   _____Dollars ($_____). The purchase price shall be paid by Buyer as follows:
   (a) Buyer shall pay to Seller or Seller's agent, upon signing this Agreement, the amount of _____
   _____Dollars ($_____) by cash or check as a deposit in escrow to be applied toward the purchase price.
   (b) Buyer shall pay to Seller or Seller's agent, on or before the closing date of this Agreement, the balance of the purchase
   price in the amount of _____ Dollars ($_____) by cash or certified check.

5. The closing date of this Agreement shall be on the _____ day of _____, 19___, at the time of_____
   and at the place of _____.
   Time is of the essence for the closing of this Agreement.

6. This Agreement is contingent upon Buyer obtaining a mortgage commitment by the ___ day of _____ , 19___ from a regular lending institution for a mortgage loan on the following terms:

        (a) minimum amount of mortgage loan: $_____

        (b) maximum annual interest rate: _____%

        (c) maximum loan fee or points: _____%

        (d) minimum term of mortgage: _____ years

Buyer shall exercise reasonable and good faith efforts to obtain a mortgage commitment by the prescribed date on the above terms or more favorable ones. In the event that Buyer is unable to obtain such a mortgage commitment by the prescribed date, this Agreement shall be void and all obligations hereunder terminated, except that any funds paid by Buyer as deposits shall be returned to Buyer.

7. Seller shall convey to Buyer good, insurable and marketable title to the property by _____ deed. If Seller is to convey by warranty deed, Seller warrants title to be free and clear of all liens, charges, defects, and encumbrances, except for the conditions, restrictions, reservations, and easements listed below:

8. Seller makes the following additional representations and warranties to Buyer, which shall survive the conveyance of title to Buyer:

9. Seller shall give possession of the property to Buyer at the date of closing, and the property shall be in the condition as warranted by Seller, or in the condition as of the date of this Agreement if Seller makes no warranties as to the condition of the property.

10. The risk of loss or damage to the property shall remain with Seller until conveyance of title to Buyer. The risk of loss or damage to the Property shall be with Buyer after conveyance of title to Buyer.

11. Any prepaid utilities and any real estate taxes shall be pro rated as of the date of closing. Seller shall be responsible for any such utilities and taxes up to and including the date of closing and Buyer shall be responsible for any such utilities and taxes thereafter.

12. Seller shall be responsible for payment of any commission to any real estate agent or broker involved in procuring the sale of this property.

13. This Agreement shall be governed by the laws of the State of _____.

14. This Agreement shall be binding upon and inure to the benefit of Buyer and Seller and their respective heirs, successors, and assigns.

Buyer and Seller, intending to be legally bound, have signed this Agreement on the date first indicated above.

_____   _____
Buyer's Signature   Seller's Signature

_____   _____
Witness' Signature   Witness' Signature

Promissory Note

Amount $_____

Date _____

1. I, _____(Maker's name)

_____(Maker's address),

for valuable and sufficient consideration received, promise to pay to the order of

_____(Payee's name)

_____(Payee's address)

the sum of _____ Dollars ($_____), along with interest from the date of this Note on

the unpaid principal at an annual rate of _____ percent (_____%).

2. **(a)** Principal and interest due under this note shall be payable as follows:

(b) Payments due under this Note shall be made at the following address or as Payee or assigns may reasonably designate:

3. Default in the payment of any amount when due as provided in this Note, or the voluntary or involuntary filing of a petition for bankruptcy of Maker, shall at the discretion of the Payee or assigns, cause the entire unpaid balance hereof to become immediately due and payable. If collection efforts have to be made to enforce payment of any amount due under this note, Maker shall pay all reasonable costs and attorney fees incurred in such collection.

4. Maker may prepay the principal balance and interest due under this note at any time in whole or in part without incurring any penalties.

5. Maker gives the following property as collateral security for the payment of this note, and shall execute any necessary documents to perfect said security interest:

6. This note shall be governed by the laws of the State of _____.

Maker, intending to be legally bound, has signed this Promissory Note on this _____ day of _____, 19___.

_____
Maker's signature

Subscribed and sworn to before me on this _____ day of _____, 19___.

_____
Notary

General Warranty Deed

1. By this General Warranty Deed made on this ____ day of _____, 19____

    I, _____(Grantor's name)

    _____(Grantor's address)

    hereby give, grant, transfer and convey to

    _____(Grantee's name)

    _____(Grantee's address),

    and Grantee's heirs and assigns in fee simple, the real property, including the land and all the buildings and structures on

    the land, located at _____(address of property),

    and legally described as:

2. This conveyance is made in consideration for the sum of _____ Dollars ($_____)

    paid to and received by Grantor.

3. Grantor and Grantor's heirs hereby warrant that Grantor has good and legal title to the above-described property, that Grantor

    has a good right to convey, that said property is free of all encumbrances except those of record and specified herein, and

    that Grantor and Grantor's heirs will defend said property against every person claiming the same.

    In Witness Whereof, the Grantor has signed this General Warranty Deed on the date first described above.

    _____
    Grantor's Signature

Witnessed By:

_____   _____
Witness' Signature   Witness' Signature

_____   _____
Witness' Address   Witness' Address

Subscribed and sworn to before me on this ____ day of _____, 19____.

_____
Notary

Deed   **Recorded At:**

_____,
Grantor

To

_____
Grantee

Special Warranty Deed

1. By this Special Warranty Deed made on this ____ day of _____, 19____

   I, _____(Grantor's name)

   _____(Grantor's address)

   hereby give, grant, transfer and convey to

   _____(Grantee's name)

   _____(Grantee's address),

   and Grantee's heirs and assigns in fee simple, the real property, including the land and all the buildings and structures on

   the land, located at _____(address of property),

   and legally described as:

2. This conveyance is made in consideration for the sum of _____ Dollars ($_____)

   paid to and received by Grantor.

3. Grantor and Grantor's heirs hereby warrant that they have not done anything to destroy or otherwise affect good and legal

   title to the above-described property or Grantor's right to convey, that said property is free of all encumbrances except those

   of record and specified herein, and that Grantor and Grantor's heirs will defend said property against every person claiming

   the same by, through, or under Grantor and Grantor's heirs.

In Witness Whereof, the Grantor has signed this Special Warranty Deed on the date first described above.

_____
Grantor's Signature

Witnessed By:

_____   _____
Witness' Signature   Witness' Signature

_____   _____
Witness' Address   Witness' Address

Subscribed and sworn to before me on this ____ day of _____, 19____.

_____
Notary

Deed   **Recorded At:**

_____
Grantor

To

_____
Grantee

Quitclaim Deed

1. By this Quitclaim Deed made on this _____ day of _____, 19_____,
   I, _____ (Grantor's name)
   _____ (Grantor's address)
   hereby give, grant, transfer, convey and quitclaim to

   _____ (Grantee's name)

   _____ (Grantee's address)
   and Grantee's heirs and assigns, any and all of Grantor's rights, title, and interest in and to the real property, including the land and all the buildings and structures on the land, located at

   _____ (address of property),
   and legally described as:

2. This conveyance is made in consideration for the sum of _____ (Dollars ($_____)
   paid to and received by Grantor.

In Witness Whereof, the Grantor has signed this Quitclaim Deed on the date first described above.

_____
Grantor's Signature

Witnessed By:

_____   _____
Witness' Signature   Witness' Signature

_____   _____
Witness' Address   Witness' Address

Subscribed and sworn to before me on this ____ day of _____, 19____.

_____
Notary

Deed   **Recorded At:**

_____
Grantor

To

_____
Grantee

11 *Leasing Your Home or Office*

Looking at Renting

In many cases, renting can be a reasonable alternative to buying a home or commercial property. For many young adults, renting an apartment or house may be the only means to obtain affordable housing. Likewise, renting an office or commercial space may be the only route for a young professional or small business to get started. Having a good understanding of the landlord-tenant relationship and resources available can be beneficial to both the prospective tenant and landlord.

Many resources may be available to you if you are trying to find rental property. They may also be useful if you own real estate and will be holding it as investment rental property. These sources of information and assistance include the newspapers, community agencies, business associations, rental agencies, real estate agencies, and employer personnel and relocation departments.

The rental process typically starts with the interested tenant inspecting premises which the landlord has listed or advertised for rent. It is at this time that the tenant should make a careful inspection and examination of the rental premises for suitability for his or her particular needs. If the premises are acceptable, the tenant and landlord typically negotiate and sign a lease agreement.

For many residential leases, the prospective tenant is initially required to complete an application form and give information on his or her background and financial status. Similar credit and financial information may be required for commercial leases. The tenant is required to pay a nonrefundable application fee which can range from about $20 to $100. If the prospective tenant's credit and financial and other background are acceptable, the tenant and landlord then proceed with executing a lease agreement.

The lease agreement should always be in writing with the terms of the lease clearly spelled out. Although oral leases are generally valid, you should never enter into an oral lease. Your lease must be in writing if it has a rental period of more than one year. Even if the rental period is one year or less, the lease must still be in writing if any portion of the rental period will extend beyond one year after the lease has been fully signed. For example, if you enter into a lease agreement today for a six-month lease which will start seven months in the future, the lease generally must be in writing. Both the tenant and the landlord should always read and understand the lease before signing it.

The tenant is usually required to pay the first month's rent and a security deposit equal to one to two months' rent upon signing the lease. The security deposit (which is discussed later in this chapter) is refunded to the tenant after appropriate deductions for damages and other charges after expiration of the lease.

The tenant usually receives the keys and possession of the premises after the lease has been fully executed and the landlord-tenant relationship has begun. Legal fees for simple landlord-tenant cases typically range from about $200 to $1000.

Understanding Landlord-Tenant Law

The landlord-tenant relationship is primarily contractual and results from a lease of real estate for a term of years, from period to period, for life, or at will. Basically, a landlord-tenant relationship exists anytime a person occupies and has possession of the premises of another person with the other's permission.

Landlord-tenant relationships are governed by concepts of both contract law and property law. A lease of real estate creates a contract between the lessor (landlord) and the lessee (tenant) in which responsibilities and obligations are imposed on both parties. The obligations under contract law are generally determined by the terms of the lease agreement.

Since a lease is a conveyance of an interest in real estate, principles of property law may come into play. A lease typically conveys to the tenant the right to exclusive possession of the premises in exchange for the tenant's obligation to pay rent. It is important that the lease refer to specific premises at a fixed location to avoid ambiguities.

Historically, property laws did not excuse a tenant from the obligation to pay rent if the landlord failed to maintain the premises or otherwise breached the lease. This situation has been changed recently in many states, where a tenant of residential property generally receives an implied warranty of habitability which is tied to the obligation to pay rent.

Types of Landlord-Tenant Relationships

There are four basic leasehold tenancies created by the landlord-tenant relationship. These tenancies are as follows:

- Periodic Tenancy. A periodic tenancy is one for a repeated period of time that has no specific termination date. An example would be a month-to-month lease. This tenancy is automatically renewed from period to period and can only be terminated by proper notice from the landlord or the tenant. Proper notice is usually required to be at least one period under the lease. For example, for a month-to-month lease, at least one month notice of termination is normally required.

- Tenancy for Years. A tenancy for years is created by a lease for a fixed period of time and with a definite termination date. It can be for more or less than a year. Examples would be a 6-month or a 1-year lease. No notice of termination is usually required unless specified by the lease agreement. A tenancy for years automatically terminates upon expiration of the lease, unless the landlord and tenant have agreed to extend the lease. The typical residential lease is for a fixed period and may provide that the lease will be automatically extended for a similar fixed period unless notice of termination is given one to three months before expiration of the lease.

- Tenancy at Will. A tenancy at will exists when either the landlord or the tenant has the right to terminate the lease at will and at any time. The tenancy at will is not common because it offers no stability to either the tenant or the landlord. Notice of termination is required to terminate a tenancy at will. Some states may require a minimum of one-month notice of termination even for a tenancy at will.

- Tenancy at Sufferance. A tenancy at sufferance or holdover tenancy exists when the tenant fails or refuses to vacate after the expiration of the lease. In such a case, the landlord may treat the tenant as a trespasser and seek eviction or the landlord may choose to hold the tenant to a new tenancy under the old lease.

You should choose the leasing arrangement which is best for your particular circumstances. The tenancy for years or fixed period is appropriate in most residential and commercial situations. It offers stability in both duration of the lease and in the amount of rent. A month-to-month tenancy may be appropriate when the rental property is on the market for sale or when the tenant expects to relocate in the near future.

Warranty of Habitability

For hundred of years, the landlord had no duty to deliver or maintain the rented premises in a condition of habitability or fitness for any purpose, unless this duty was explicitly included in the terms of the lease agreement. Landlord-tenant law has been changed in many states to impose greater responsibilities on the landlord, especially in residential leases. Many states now require that residential premises comply with housing codes and occupancy standards, and recognize that residential leases contain an implied warranty of habitability. The implied warranty of habitability does not have to be written into the lease agreement, but is implied by operation of law as a required feature of residential leases.

The implied warranty of habitability requires the landlord to keep the premises in a condition that is suitable for living purposes. This usually means that the premises must comply with all housing, building, and safety codes. Minor defects in the premises do not violate the warranty of habitability. This requirement of habitability generally must be satisfied at the beginning of the lease and continues throughout the entire term of the lease. The following forty-one states have adopted the implied warranty of habitability either by legislation or court decisions:

Alaska, Arizona, California, Delaware, Florida, Georgia, Hawaii, Idaho, Illinois, Indiana, Iowa, Kansas, Kentucky, Louisiana, Maine, Maryland, Massachusetts, Michigan, Minnesota, Missouri, Montana, Nebraska, New Hampshire, New Jersey, New Mexico, New York, North Carolina, North Dakota, Ohio, Oklahoma, Oregon, Pennsylvania, Rhode Island, South Carolina, South Dakota, Tennessee, Texas, Vermont, Virginia, Washington, West Virginia, and Wisconsin.

The implied warranty of habitability generally does not extend to commercial or business-type leases.

In most cases, the tenant's obligation to pay rent under a residential lease is dependent upon the landlord's compliance with the warranty of habitability. If the landlord breaches the warranty of habitability, the tenant may terminate the lease and vacate the premises without any further obligation to pay rent. The tenant would also be entitled to recover any rent paid in advance under the lease. If the tenant chooses to remain in possession, the rent may be reduced by a percentage amount equal to that percentage of the leased premise which is in violation of the warranty of habitability. Some states also permit the tenant to remain in possession and pay rent into escrow with the court or to make the necessary repairs and deduct the costs for such repairs from the rent. In any event, the tenant usually must give notice of defects to the landlord and allow a reasonable time for the landlord to correct the defects before the tenant can withhold rent or make repairs.

The tenant can also report housing and building code violations to the proper authorities in an effort to force the landlord to make repairs. The laws typically prohibit the landlord from taking any retaliatory action against a tenant who has reported violations or withheld rent because the leased premises were uninhabitable.

It is important that good documentary evidence be maintained of communications between the tenant and landlord. Problems with maintenance and service should always be brought to the landlord's attention in writing, with the tenant keeping a copy for his or her records. Even when the tenant has discussed problems with the landlord orally or over the telephone, the tenant should follow up with a letter. The tenant should retain receipts for any repairs by the tenant to the leased premises. The tenant should also receive signed receipts from the landlord for deposits, fees, and rental payments made to the landlord. Both the tenant and the landlord should each keep a copy of the lease agreement for their respective files.

Other Landlord-Tenant Obligations

In addition to maintaining the leased premises in a habitable condition, the landlord must live up to all other requirements and conditions specified in the lease agreement. The landlord must also exercise reasonable care to keep the premises secure and free of hazards. In many states, a lease's exculpatory clauses exempting the landlord from liability for damages and injuries resulting from the landlord's negligence are invalid.

Federal and state laws generally prohibit discrimination in leases. The Federal Fair Housing Act makes it illegal to refuse to sell or rent a dwelling on the basis of race, color, religion, sex, familial status or national origin. The "familial status" prohibition was designed to eliminate discriminating against families with children, except when the housing is intended for elderly residents. A prospective tenant can bring legal action in federal or state court against the landlord for violating the Fair Housing Act.

The tenant also has obligations under a lease. The primary obligation of the tenant is the timely payment of rent. The amount, time, and place for payment of rent is usually spelled out in the lease agreement. The lease agreement may also impose additional obligations and restrictions on the tenant, such as restricting use of the premises to either residential or commercial, requiring fire insurance, restricting the number of occupants, prohibiting pets, restricting alterations to the premises, requiring tenant to maintain the premises in a clean and safe

condition, prohibiting illegal activities, and complying with housing codes and zoning laws.

If the tenant breaches important and material obligations under the lease agreement, the landlord may be able to terminate the lease. Most states provide for relatively quick judicial proceedings (typically two to four weeks) for evicting a tenant who has violated material provisions of the lease. The most common ground for termination of the lease and eviction of the tenant is nonpayment of rent. Other grounds for eviction frequently include illegal use of the leased premises, failure to maintain the premises in the condition required, unauthorized pets, and failure to comply with building and zoning regulations. The landlord may also bring legal action to collect rents and damages if the tenant has violated the lease.

The tenant also has various remedies when the landlord has violated the lease. Many of these remedies, such as termination of the lease, withholding of rent, payment of rent into escrow, reduction in rent, and deductions for repairs, were discussed earlier with respect to when the landlord has breached the warranty of habitability. The tenant may also bring legal action to recover monetary damages.

Security Deposits

It is common in both residential and commercial leases for the landlord to require that the tenant pay a security deposit. This security deposit serves as a source of funds for the landlord to resort to in case the tenant breaches the lease agreement or otherwise causes damage to the leased premises. The security deposit is normally paid to and held by the landlord until expiration of the lease.

The amount of the security deposit usually ranges from about one to three months' rent. Some states limit the amount of security deposit to no more than two months' rent. The landlord is normally free to hold the security deposit without paying any interest to the tenant. However, some states, such as New Jersey, require that the landlord keep the security deposit in a separate interest-bearing account.

Many states have passed laws designed to help the residential tenant collect the security deposit after termination or expiration of the lease. Laws governing security deposits have been enacted in Alaska, Arizona, California, Connecticut, Delaware, Florida, Hawaii, Illinois, Iowa, Kansas, Kentucky, Louisiana, Maryland, Massachusetts, Michigan, Montana, Nebraska, New Jersey, New Mexico, New York, Oregon, Pennsylvania, Rhode Island, South Carolina, Tennessee, Texas, and Virginia.

These laws typically provide that the landlord must return the security deposit to the tenant within thirty to sixty days after the end of the lease.

If the tenant has damaged the leased premises, the landlord may keep part or all of the security deposit to cover the amount of damage. In such a case, the landlord must send an itemized list of damages and deductions to the tenant. Damages to the leased premises do not include normal wear and tear, but may include cleaning and painting. The tenant can usually recover double or triple the security deposit if the landlord fails to refund the security deposit within the specified time.

Assignment and Subletting
Unless prohibited by the lease agreement, the tenant may assign all or part of his or her interest in the lease. A complete transfer of all of the tenant's remaining interest in the lease is generally considered an assignment. If the tenant transfers only a part of his or her remaining interest in the lease, the transfer is a sublease.

In an assignment, the original tenant gives up possession of the entire leased premises for the full remainder of the lease period to the new tenant/assignee. Although the new tenant/assignee becomes liable to the landlord for the payment of rent, the original tenant also remains liable

unless the landlord has definitely released the original tenant from the obligation to pay rent. If the original tenant is required to pay any rent to the landlord after an assignment of the lease, the original tenant may recover that rent from the new tenant/assignee.

A sublease is essentially a partial assignment where the new tenant/sublessee either leases a part of the leased premises, or leases the entire premises for only a part of the lease period before it reverts back to the original tenant. In a sublease, the new tenant/sublessee is not personally liable to the landlord for the payment of rent. Rather, the payment of rent remains the primary responsibility of the original tenant. However, the new tenant/sublessee is obligated to pay rent to the original tenant.

For practical reasons, most commercial tenants bargain to include the right to assign or sublet in the lease. Typically the consent of the landlord is required but must not be unreasonably withheld. The ability to assign and sublet may also be important in a residential lease if the tenant may need to move or relocate. The landlord almost always has the ability to assign the right to rental payment under a lease. The landlord may also sell the leased premises and the new owner takes the property subject to any existing lease.

Basic Provisions of a Lease Agreement
It is the lease agreement, more than anything else, which governs the relationship between landlord and tenant. The lease agreement should always be in writing. It should be carefully drafted and reviewed by both the landlord and tenant to include all important terms and conditions and to avoid ambiguities and uncertainties. Once the lease agreement is signed by the landlord and tenant, it becomes a legally binding contract.

The lease agreement should include the names and addresses of the landlord and tenant. It should include a clear and definite description of the leased premises, including address, location, size, and physical characteristics of the property. Also identify any personal property, appliances, equipment, and fixtures which are included with the leased premises.

The lease agreement should indicate the purpose of the lease and the use which the tenant is to make of the leased premises. If the lease is for residential purposes, the lease agreement will preferably include the number of or names of the people who will be occupying the premises. A commercial lease should identify the specific type of commercial or business activity which will be conducted on the leased premises.

The lease agreement should include a term or lease period which usually specifies a beginning date and an ending date. The lease agreement should include the amount and frequency of rent payments and the total amount of rent due during the term of the lease. The standard rental arrangement is the flat rate which provides for a fixed amount each month for the entire term of the lease. The lease agreement should also indicate when and where rent payments are to be made. Provisions should also be included for penalties and charges for late payment of rent.

Other provisions which are customarily included in a lease agreement include responsibilities for utilities, trash removal, maintenance and repairs, heating and air-conditioning, and insurance. Also included are provisions concerning security deposits, alterations, access to the premises, assignment and subletting, condemnation by eminent domain, and indemnification of the landlord or tenant for any damages or liabilities incurred because of the other party. These provisions can be drafted in clear and simple terms to fit your particular situation.

The lease agreement is signed by both the landlord and tenant. It is recommended that the lease agreement be notarized.

A sample lease agreement is provided at the end of this chapter.

Checklist for Making a Lease

❑ Inspection of premises by tenant.

❑ Application to enter into lease. Application fee?

❑ Background and credit check on tenant.

❑ Preparation of lease agreement:

- identification of landlord and tenant
- location and description of premises, including any fixtures, equipment, appliances, and personal property
- purpose of lease and restrictions on use
- term of lease, with beginning and ending dates
- amount of rent and time and place of payment
- utilities
- maintenance and repairs`
- security deposits
- prepaid rents
- assignment and subletting
- alterations and modifications to premises
- heating and air conditioning
- trash removal
- insurance
- access to premises by landlord
- condemnation and eminent domain
- indemnification

❑ Signing of lease agreement by landlord and tenant.

❑ Delivery of possession of the leased premises to tenant.

❑ Move-in inspection by tenant and written report of any defects and damages to landlord.

❑ Consult an attorney if the leasing arrangement involves difficult or complex issues.

Lease Agreement

1. This Lease Agreement is made this _____ day of _____ , 19_____ by and between

_____(Landlord's name)

_____(Landlord's address)

and _____(Tenant's name)

_____(Tenant's address).

2. Landlord leases and transfers possession to Tenant, for the term of this Lease Agreement, of the premises located at

_____ (Address of premises);

said premises being specifically described as follows:

3. The premises leased under this Lease Agreement shall be used by Tenant solely for the purpose of:

4. The premises leased under this Lease Agreement shall be used and occupied, in accordance with Item 3 above, only by the parties listed below:

5. This Lease Agreement shall be effective for a term of _____ months, beginning on the _____ day of _____,19_____, and ending on the _____ day of _____,19_____.

6. In consideration for this Lease Agreement and the rights hereunder, Tenant shall pay rent to Landlord during the term of this Lease Agreement in the amount of _____Dollars ($_____) per _____; for a total rent for the term in the amount of _____ Dollars ($_____).

7. Rent payments hereunder are due on _____ and shall be paid at _____ or as the Landlord may designate. If any rent due and payable hereunder is not made within _____ days after said rent shall become due, Tenant shall pay to Landlord additional charges equal to _____ Dollars ($_____) for each _____ said rent remains unpaid.

8. On or before the start of the term of this Lease Agreement, Tenant shall deposit with Landlord the sum of _____ Dollars ($_____) as a security deposit for the compliance with and performance of the terms and provisions of this Lease Agreement. If Tenant should default or breach any of the terms and provisions of this lease, or has otherwise caused damage to the leased premises except for normal wear and tear, Landlord may apply, use, or keep all or part of said security deposit to the extent required to correct such default, breach, or damage.

9. The following equipment, appliances, or other personal property is included and forms a part of the leased premises under this Lease Agreement:

10. Landlord shall provide and be responsible for, at no additional cost to Tenant, the following services and utilities for the leased premises:

11. Tenant shall provide and be responsible for, at no additional cost to Landlord, the following services and utilities for the leased premises:

12. This Lease Agreement shall terminate if all or any part of the leased premises should be acquired or condemned by Eminent Domain.

13. Landlord shall have the right to enter the leased premises at reasonable times and after giving reasonable notice to Tenant to inspect, repair, or improve the leased premises or to respond to any emergency.

14. Tenant shall not assign or sublet Tenant's interest under this Lease Agreement without the prior written consent of Landlord, which consent shall not be unreasonably withheld by Landlord.

15. Landlord and Tenant agree to the following additional covenants, rules, and conditions:

16. The terms, provisions, and covenants contained in this Lease Agreement shall be binding on and inure to the benefit of Landlord and Tenant and their respective successors, heirs, and assigns.

17. This Lease Agreement shall be governed by the laws of the State of _____.

Landlord and Tenant, intending to be legally bound, have signed this Lease Agreement on the date first indicated above.

_____
Landlord's Signature

_____
Witness' Signature

_____
Witness' Address

_____
Tenant's Signature

_____
Witness' Signature

_____
Witness' Address

Subscribed and sworn to before me on this _____ day of_____,19_____.

_____
Notary

Chapter

12 *Personal Property for Sale*

Buying and Selling Personal Property

Tangible personal property, such as automobiles, boats, equipment, furniture, and appliances, is bought and sold all the time. When major items such as these are purchased from a regular business establishment they are usually accompanied by a sales receipt, invoice, or other evidence of the sale. This evidence of sale can be very important in proving ownership and for insurance purposes. It is recommended that you keep these for your records during the useful life of the property.

Likewise, when you buy and sell personal property in an informal and nonbusiness context, this transaction should be evidenced by a "bill of sale" or other appropriate documentation. A bill of sale is basically a written document which shows that a sale has taken place. It may also include important terms and conditions of the sale.

The bill of sale should identify the seller and buyer and give their respective addresses. It should contain a description of the property which is sufficient to specifically identify the property. The description should include the manufacturer's name, serial number, and date or year of manufacture, if available. The amount that the property is being sold for should also be in the bill of sale. This figure could be useful in establishing the value of the property for an insurance claim or tax loss. The bill of sale should be signed and dated by the seller. It

should also be accepted and signed by the buyer.

Other provisions that you may want to put in the bill of sale are any warranties or guarantees, terms of payment, time and place of delivery, insurance, storage, and terms for return or credit. If the seller is financing the purchase of the property, the buyer may be required to sign a promissory note. A sample promissory note is provided at the end of Chapter 10 and is useful and handy anytime you lend money or extend credit to someone.

It is common for property to be sold among family, friends, and other individuals without any warranties or guarantees. If the property is sold without any warranties, the bill of sale should indicate that it is being sold "as is" or other similar language. If the seller offers a warranty, it should be expressly written into the bill of sale with all its terms and conditions. It is common for the bill of sale to include a warranty that the Seller owns good title to the property and has the lawful right to transfer title.

Remember that you can only sell what you own. If you are selling property which is covered by a mortgage or security interest, your buyer generally acquires the property subject to these existing claims. If you own the property jointly with other people, these people must also sign the bill of sale to transfer complete title and ownership.

A sample bill of sale is provided at the end of this chapter. This bill of sale should be useful in any state to transfer ownership of most tangible personal property. Some property, such as an automobile, has an official Certificate of Title issued by the state where it is registered. In most cases this Certificate of Title must be transferred to the new owner. A bill of sale can also be used along with the Certificate of Title to include important terms and conditions.

Bill of Sale

1. By this Bill of Sale made on this _____ day of _____, 19_____,
   _____(Seller's name)
   _____(Seller's address
   hereby sells and transfers to _____(Buyer's name)
   _____(Buyer's address),
   the property described below:

2. The purchase price of the Property is _____ Dollars ($_____),
   which shall be paid by Buyer as follows:

3. Seller warrants that Seller has good title to the Property and the lawful right to sell and transfer the Property to Buyer, and that the Property is free of all liens and encumbrances, except the following:

4. Seller makes no warranties as to the condition of the Property, including no **warranty of merchantability** and no **warranty of fitness for a particular purpose,** except for any warranties expressly indicated below:

5. Additional Terms and Conditions:

Buyer and Seller, intending to be legally bound, have signed this Agreement on the date first indicated above.

_____   _____
Seller's Signature   Buyer's Signature

Subscribed and sworn to before me on this _____ day of _____,19_____.

_____
Notary

Chapter

13 Contracting for Repairs and Services

Entering into a Contract for Services

It is common for contracts to be entered into for performing a variety of personal services, such as home repairs, landscaping and gardening, equipment repairs, child care, legal services, catering, management and sale of real estate, and many others. Whether you are the provider or the recipient of these services, you should put the contract in writing to spell out clearly the obligations and terms of performance.

In Chapter 2, a lawyer's retainer agreement is reviewed, along with other considerations for hiring a lawyer. Also, a real estate listing agreement is discussed in Chapter 10 for using a real estate agent or broker in selling real property. Many of the considerations in hiring a lawyer or real estate agent are applicable in contracting for other services.

Typically, a decision has to be made whether the person to perform services will be an employee or independent contractor. It is usually less complicated and less expensive to contract for the services of an independent contractor rather than an employee. This is because an employer may be required to pay federal social security taxes and state worker's compensation insurance, withhold federal and state income tax, and provide other benefits such as health care and vacation to employees. In an employer-employee relationship, the employer may also be liable to others for any damage or injury caused by the em-

ployee during the course of the employment. Most of these problems can be avoided by contracting with an independent contractor.

A contract for the services of an independent contractor should clearly indicate that the person performing the services is an independent contractor and not an employee. The contract should identify the contractor along with the contractor's address. It should also include the customer's name and address.

The contract should include a complete description of the work and duties which are to be performed by the independent contractor. Be sure to include the time period within which the services of the contractor are to be completed. If the time for completing the work is of critical importance, then the contract should provide that time is of the essence.

The contract should include the amount and manner of compensation to be paid to the independent contractor. This can be a fixed amount — typically payable in installments during the course of the work — or a total sum to be paid when the work is completed. Many contractors may charge an hourly or daily rate for their services. In any event, try to put in the contract a good faith estimate of costs, and indicate whether this includes any materials and expenses as well as services.

Include in the contract any warranties and guarantees of performance from the contractor. The contractor should be responsible for hiring any assistants needed and should indemnify the customer for liability caused by the contractor, assistants, or the contractor's subcontractors (if any). It is recommended that some provision be included in the contract for termination.

It is common for the contract to be terminated by the customer for nonperformance or breach by the contractor. The contractor typically can terminate the contract for nonpayment or noncooperation.

Other provisions may be included in the contract for services, such as delegation and assignment, penalties for nonperformance, insurance, and other restrictions and requirements. The contract is signed by both the contractor and the customer.

A sample Contract for Services is provided at the end of this chapter. Attorney's fees for drafting a simple contract range from about $100 to $300 depending on complexity and location.

Contract for Services

1. This Contract for Services is made on this _____ day of _____,19_____ by and between
_____(Contractor's name)
_____(Contractor's address)
and _____(Customer's name)
_____(Customer's address).

2. Contractor shall perform the following work, duties, or services on behalf of Customer in a professional and workmanlike manner:

3. Customer shall pay to Contractor, for the work, duties, or services performed under this contract, compensation in the amount of and at the time as provided below:

4. The work, duties, or services to be performed by Contractor under this Contract shall commence on the _____ day of _____,19____ and shall be completed on the _____ day of _____,19___. Time is of the essence for the performance under this Contract.

5. Contractor is and shall remain an independent contractor at all times under this Contract. Contractor shall be responsible for hiring any assistants or subcontractors needed in performing under this Contract at no additional cost to Customer. Contractor shall indemnify Customer for any and all damages and liabilities caused by Contractor or Contractor's subcontractors or assistants in their performance under this Contract.

6. This Contract can be terminated as provided below:

7. This Contract shall be binding on and inure to the benefit of Contractor, Customer and their respective heirs, successors and assigns.

8. This Contract shall not be assigned, nor any performance hereunder delegated by Contractor or Customer, without the express written consent of the other, which consent shall not be unreasonably withheld.

9. Additional Terms and Conditions:

10. This Contract shall be governed by the laws of the State of _____.

Contractor and Customer, intending to be legally bound, have signed this Contract as of the date first set forth above.

_____   _____
            Contractor's Signature   Customer's Signature

Subscribed and sworn to before me on this _____ day of _____,19_____.

_____
                    Notary

14 Handling a Simple Divorce or Separation

What to Do When Relationships Don't Work

Practically everyone has been in a personal romantic relationship of some type that has not worked out. Typically these relationships end on a bitter note because of inflamed emotions, disappointments, accusations of fault and other conflicts. However, relationships do not have to end in such a negative fashion, if you and your partner work at conciliation and compromise for a positive resolution.

Many times in a personal relationship, your emotions may cloud your judgment and your ability to settle issues on an amicable basis. Most people just never learn how to manage their personal relationships, nor how to plan in the event that they come to an end. Rather, we spend most of our lives focusing on our jobs and careers and so little time focusing on our personal relationships. Although there is no magic formula for a happy marriage or relationship, or a happy ending to one, you can typically foster such positive results by communication, compromise, and planning.

If the relationship is important to you, try sincere efforts to make it work. Talk over problems with your spouse or partner. Ask close friends and family for advice and counseling without making your friends and family an issue in the relationship. Consider obtaining the help of a marriage counselor or other professional mediator to help the two of you identify problems and potential solutions.

It is important that you be fair and honest to yourself and your spouse or partner. Realize that relationships don't always last despite your best efforts to make the relationship survive. Talk to each other about what should happen if the relationship ends. Don't focus on fault and blame as this can be counterproductive. Rather, look at what can be a win-win situation for both of you. Also consider what's best for any children involved. Both of you can learn and grow from even a failed relationship.

Property Settlement and Other Agreements

Many times, a fair and equitable separation, property settlement, or prenuptial agreement can be helpful in making a break up amicable. These agreements have been frequently criticized because it is said that they take the romance out of the relationship. But these agreements can do much to relieve tension and promote harmony in the relationship.

A prenuptial agreement is basically a property settlement agreement, entered into by prospective spouses prior to marriage, which provides for the property rights of one or both of the prospective spouses and/or any children. These agreements are recognized and enforced in many, but not all, of the states. Generally, a prenuptial property settlement agreement must be in writing and signed by both parties. A prenuptial agreement can define the rights and obligations of each of the parties in any of the property of either of them, whenever and wherever acquired or located. You can also agree to your rights to buy, sell, use, transfer or otherwise manage and control property. You can provide for the disposition of property upon separation, marriage dissolution, death, or the occurrence or non-occurrence of any other event. Additionally, you may eliminate or modify any obligations of spousal support.

A sample property settlement agreement is provided at the end of this chapter. This agreement may be useful as a prenuptial agreement in contemplation of marriage to settle property, support, custody, and other issues. You may also find the property settlement agreement useful if you are going through a separation or divorce.

It may even be beneficial for couples who will only be living and cohabiting together to enter into a property settlement agreement. Often times couples living together contribute jointly to the acquisition of furniture, household items and other assets. It is recommended that couples living together enter into a property settlement agreement to address ownership of property and other rights. The sample property settlement agreement provided at the end of this chapter is also useful for couples who plan to live together.

Going Through a Divorce

Going through a divorce is never easy. But if your marriage is irretrievably broken, a divorce may be the best way to terminate the relationship and start life anew.

Many states now allow a divorce based on consent and commonly called "no fault" divorce. This approach can foster an amicable divorce in which both spouses agree that the marriage has broken down. Some states allow a divorce when there has been a separation and the husband and wife have lived apart for a specified period of time.

You can also obtain a divorce based on fault, but these tend to be complicated and unfriendly. It is recommended that you obtain legal counsel if you are undergoing a complicated or contested divorce. Typical legal fees for a simple divorce range from about $300 to $1000, depending on complexity and location.

Typical grounds for a divorce based on fault include adultery, willful desertion, physical cruelty, insanity, habitual drunkeness, and conviction of a felony. Adultery is usually defined as a voluntary sexual relationship with another person, other than a spouse and without the spouse's consent. Desertion is the intentional abandonment of marital cohabitation by either spouse without cause or justification and without the consent of the abandoned spouse. Physical cruelty involves personal violence and physical treatment that endangers life, limb, or health and renders cohabitatin unsafe.

Habitual drunkeness typically involves a frequent state of intoxication for a specific period to time such as one or two years. Insanity generally requires a mental disease, defect, or failure of the mind such that a spouse does not have the capacity to conduct his or her own affairs. The felony conviction as a basis for divorce typically requires a prison sentence for a specified period of time.

Basically, a divorce is the legal termination of a marriage resulting from a court decree. Divorce laws may vary significantly from state to state. Be sure to check the specific rules and requirements for your particular state.

A divorce differs from an annulment. A divorce terminates a valid marriage. An annulment declares the marriage completely void because of some defect or disability, so from the legal viewpoint the marriage never took place.

Most states require specific periods of residence in the particular state before its courts can grant a divorce. These residency requirements may be as long as one year. Again, check the requirements in your state.

A state has jurisdiction to grant a divorce to a resident, even if the other spouse lives outside that state. However, if the court does not have personal jurisdiction over the nonresident spouse, the divorce decree normally may not provide for alimony payments or division of property.

A divorce properly obtained in one state must be honored and given full faith in other states. This recognition of out-of-state divorces is required by the federal Constitution. No such recognition and full faith is required for divorces granted in foreign countries. However, most states recognize divorces of foreign countries if at least one spouse resided in the foreign country.

An action for divorce is commenced by one spouse filing a complaint for divorce with the court. Divorce actions are typically brought in the family court for your jurisdiction. A sample Complaint for Divorce is provided at the end of this chapter. This complaint should be useful in most states, particularly in filing for a "no fault" or "mutual consent" divorce.

The Complaint for Divorce identifies the plaintiff (spouse filing for divorce) and defendant (spouse who is being sued) in the left caption. The court and docket number are usually placed in the right caption. The complaint must generally include specific allegations as to jurisdiction, residence, date and place of marriage, and basis for divorce. Other declarations and requests may be included concerning other court actions, children, custody, visitation, property settlement agreements, support, and alimony. The complaint concludes with a request for a judgment dissolving the marriage and any further relief sought. The complaint typically must be signed and dated by the plaintiff.

It may be required that the complaint for divorce be verified by a sworn affidavit signed by the plaintiff. Some states may also require that an affidavit of consent, signed by both spouses, be filed with the complaint for "no fault" or "mutual consent" divorces. A sample Affidavit of Consent is provided at the end of this chapter. Some states, such as Pennsylvania, may also require that special notices to defend and claim rights be filed.

You file a divorce complaint and other required documents with the appropriate court in your jurisdiction. An original copy of your marriage license should be attached to the complaint. Filing fees are typically required and vary for each jurisdiction. Always keep a copy of the complaint for your records and obtain the docket number for your case from the court clerk.

A copy of the complaint must generally be served on the defendant. Service of the complaint upon your defendant spouse is normally accomplished by you or the court through personal service or by certified mail. If the defendant's address and location are unknown, you may be required to advertise the divorce action in the newspaper at your locality and the last known locality of the defendant.

The court normally sets a date for a hearing in the case which usually must be attended by you and the defendant or legal counsel. If the defendant spouse fails to respond or appear, after proper service of the complaint, the court may nevertheless grant a divorce decree by default. If you, the plaintiff, fail to appear, the court may dismiss the case.

If the court is satisfied that all legal requirements have been met, it will issue a decree for divorce and other appropriate relief.

Checklist for Filing for a Simple Divorce

❑ Try efforts at reconciliation, if possible.

❑ Negotiate a property settlement agreement, if possible.

❑ Prepare Complaint for Divorce.

❑ Attach original copy of marriage license.

❏ Attach a copy of property settlement agreement, if any.

❏ Check residency requirements for your state.

❏ Prepare an Affidavit of Consent if required in your state for "no fault" or "mutual consent" divorces.

❏ Check with Court Clerk for filing fees and requirements in your state.

❏ File Complaint for Divorce and any accompanying documents with court clerk. Obtain docket number from court clerk.

❏ Serve complaint on defendant spouse.

❏ Attend hearings as required by the court.

❏ Consult an attorney if your divorce involves complex or complicated issues.

Property Settlement Agreement

1. This Agreement is made this _____ day of_____,19_____
    by and between _____(First Party's Name)
    _____(First Party's Address)
    and _____(Second Party's Name)
    _____(Second Party's Address).

2. For and in consideration of the mutual covenants, promises, and acts to be performed by each party hereunder, the parties hereby agree to the terms and conditions of this Agreement, and that this Agreement shall be binding as the final disposition of any and all property, spousal, marital, parental, and custody rights and obligations between the parties.

3. The First Party shall have exclusive rights to and ownership of the property listed below whenever and wherever acquired or located:

4. The Second Party shall have exclusive rights to and ownership of the property listed below whenever and wherever acquired or located:

5. Except as otherwise provided in this Agreement, each party may dispose of his or her property in any way, and each party hereby waives and relinquishes any and all rights to share in the property or the estate of the other as a result of marriage, cohabitation, joint tenancy, or any other relationship.

6. The First Party shall have the obligations of and be responsible for the following:

7. The Second Party shall have the obligations of and be responsible for the following:

8. The custody of any minor children of the parties shall be as follows:

9. Each of the parties shall, at the request and expense of the other party, acknowledge, execute, sign and deliver to the other party any documents which may be required to bring into effect the property rights and other interests and provisions of this Agreement.

10. The parties agree to the following additional terms and conditions:

11. This Agreement contains the entire understanding and agreement between the parties, and shall be binding on and inure to the benefit of the parties and their respective heirs, successors, and assigns.

12. This Agreement shall be governed by the laws of the State of _____.

13. This Agreement shall remain in effect until expressly terminated in writing by mutual agreement of the parties.

The First Party and Second Party, intending to be legally bound, have signed this Agreement below of their own free will as of the date first set forth above.

_____   _____
First Party's Signature   Second Party's Signature

Subscribed and sworn to before me on this _____ day of _____, 19_____.

_____
Notary

Complaint for Divorce

_____
Plaintiff

v.

_____
Defendant

Court _____

Docket No. _____

The plaintiff, _____, respectfully declares the following:

1. Plaintiff currently resides at the following address: _____
   _____

2. Plaintiff has been a resident of the State of _____ for a period of _____ months.

3. Defendant currently resides at the following address: _____
   _____

4. Plaintiff and Defendant were married on the _____ day of_____, 19_____ and at the place of
   _____(city) _____(county) _____(state). A copy of the
   marriage license is attached hereto.

5. Plaintiff seeks a divorce from Defendant based on the following:

6. There have been no previous actions for divorce or annulment between Plaintiff and Defendant except:

7. The marriage between Plaintiff and Defendant is irretrievably broken and efforts at reconciliation have not been successful.

8. Plaintiff and Defendant ____ have (copy attached) ____ have not entered into a Settlement Agreement.

9. Other declarations:

Wherefore, Plaintiff requests judgment dissolving the marriage between the parties and such further relief as Plaintiff may have requested herein.

Verification

I, being of full age and mind, hereby certify that I am the Plaintiff in the foregoing Complaint for Divorce, that all declarations are true to the best of my knowledge and belief, and that said Complaint is filed in good faith and without collusion. I am aware that perjury and willful false statements will subject me to punishment under the law.

_____   _____
Plaintiff's Signature   Date

_____   _____
Address   Telephone

Subscribed and sworn to before me on this ____ day of_____, 19_____.

_____
Notary

Affidavit of Consent

_____
            Plaintiff

                v.

_____
            Defendant

Court _____

Docket No. _____

1. A Complaint for Divorce was filed between Plaintiff and Defendant on the _____ day of _____, 19_____.

2. The marriage between Plaintiff and Defendant is irretrievably broken and efforts at reconciliation have failed.

3. I, _____, consent to the entry of a final judgment dissolving the marriage between Plaintiff and Defendant and such further relief as requested in the Complaint for Divorce.

4. I hereby certify that all statements made in this Affidavit of Consent are true to the best of my knowledge and belief. I am aware that perjury and willful false statements will subject me to punishment under the law.

_____
            Signature

_____
            Date

Subscribed and sworn to before me on this _____ day of _____, 19_____.

_____
            Notary

Chapter

15 *Getting a New Name*

What's in a Name?

Your name is the designation by which you are known in the community in which you live and work. It is what distinguishes you from other people. At law, it is also the designation by which you become bound in contracts and other legal documents.

A legal name basically consists of a given first name (such as Dyan) and a surname (such as Bryson). This name is generally given at birth and may include one or more middle names or initials. Middle names and initials may not be recognized as part of the legal name in some states. Likewise, designations such as Sr., Jr., Dr., Mr., or Mrs. do not normally constitute a part of a legal name.

A name must normally consist of words and letters. Numerals, such as 1, 2 or 3, generally are not included as part of a name.

A married woman normally retains the right to use her maiden name and she is not required to adopt the name of her husband. This may be important to a woman who has developed a longstanding professional use of her maiden name. Thus, a married woman may adopt her husband's surname as a matter of custom rather than as a matter of law.

Historically, a person was free to adopt and use any name he or she desired as long as it was not done for fraud and did not interfere with the rights of others. The person would be legally bound by any contract or other agreement into which he or she en-

tered under the adopted name. Also, the person could normally sue and be sued in the adopted name.

Your signature is any mark used to represent your name and intended to operate as your signature. Your signature does not have to be a full expression of your legal name, but can include abbreviations, initials, nicknames, or any other mark intended by you as your signature.

Changing Your Name

At common law, you could change your name at will merely by using a new name. However, most states have enacted laws which provide rules and procedures for officially changing your name. These laws typically require that you file an application or petition for a name change with the proper court.

The petition to change your name must generally be in writing and filed with the court in the county where you reside. The petition normally includes your name, address, age, place of birth, marital status, and your proposed new name. You may also be required to include all names you have used in the past five to ten years, any pending legal actions and outstanding judgments, any criminal convictions, and the names and addresses of any creditors. The petition usually includes reasons for the change of name, which can be any lawful purpose. It is normally a sufficient reason that you like the new name better because of social, religious, or any other reason that you feel is a benefit. The petition usually must be signed by you as the petitioner and may require a sworn verification as to the truth of any statements made in the petition.

You can also file a petition to change the name of any of your minor children. Some states require that if both parents are living, both must sign the petition to change the name of a minor child. However, some states allow a single parent to petition for a name change for a child without the other parent's consent. Courts usually look at what would be in the best interests of the child in granting a petition to change the child's name.

A sample Petition to Change Name and Petition to Change Name of Minor Child are provided at the end of this chapter. The petition should be filed with the appropriate court along with any required filing fees. In most cases you are required to publish notice of your petition for a name change in a newspaper of general circulation in your area. Check with the court clerk in your jurisdiction for specific requirements.

After the petition has been filed, the court will normally schedule a hearing to decide the issue. Generally, the court will grant the petition to change the name unless someone has a justifiable objection, the legal requirements have not been met, or the petition was filed with intent to defraud or other unlawful purposes. After the petition for a name change has been granted, you generally must be known and referred to by the new name only.

You should consult an attorney if your name change involves difficult or complex issues. Typical legal fees for a simple name change range from about $300 to $1,000.

**Checklist for
Filing Petition to Change Name**

❏ Choose the new name.

❏ Prepare Petition to Change Name. If you are seeking to change the name of a mi-

nor child, prepare Petition to Change Name of Minor Child.

❏ Attach a copy of your birth certificate to petition. For a minor child, attach a copy of the child's birth certificate to the petition.

❏ Attach a Consent to Name Change signed by the other parent or child, if required.

❏ Sign and date the petition. Include a Verification, if required.

❏ Check with court clerk for filing fees and other requirements.

❏ File petition and other required documents with the court. Obtain docket number from court clerk.

❏ Publish notice of petition to change name in local newspaper.

❏ Attend hearings as required by the court.

❏ Court grants your petition to change name.

❏ Start using your new name only.

❏ Consult an attorney if your name change involves difficult or complex issues.

Petition to Change Name

Petitioner's Name _____   Court _____

                                                        Docket No. _____

In re: Name Change From: _____

                    To: _____

Petitioner hereby declares the following:

1. Petitioner resides at the following address: _____

_____

2. Petitioner has resided at the above address for _____ months.

3. Petitioner was born on the ____ day of _____, 19____ at the place of _____(city)

_____(county)_____(state). A certified copy of petitioner's birth

certificate is attached hereto.

4. Petitioner was named _____ at birth and had always been known by that name,

except for the following:

5. The name of petitioner's father is _____, who resides at the following

address _____

6. The name of petitioner's mother is _____, who resides at the following

address _____

7. Petitioner desires a change of name to _____ for the following
reason(s):

8. Other declarations:

Wherefore, petitioner requests the court to issue an order changing petitioner's name

from _____

to _____

Verification

I, _____, hereby certify that I am the petitioner in the foregoing Petition to Change
Name, that all statements made herein are true to the best of my knowledge and belief. I am aware that perjury and willful false
statements will subject me to punishment under the law.

_____   _____
Petitioner's Signature   Date

_____   _____
Address   Telephone

Subscribed and sworn to before me on this _____ day of_____, 19_____.

_____
Notary

Petition to Change Name of Minor Child

Petitioner's Name(s) _____   Court _____

_____   Docket No. _____

In re: Name Change of Minor Child

From: _____

To: _____

Petitioner(s) hereby declare(s) the following:

1. Petitioner(s) reside(s) at the following address _____

2. Petitioner(s) has/have resided at the above address for _____ months.

3. On the _____ day of _____, 19_____, a minor child named _____ was born to petitioner(s). A certified copy of the birth certificate of said minor child is attached hereto.

4. Said minor child resides at the following address _____

5. Petitioner(s) desire(s) to change the name of said minor child from _____ to _____ for the following reason(s):

6. Other declarations:

Wherefore, petitioner(s) request(s) the court to issue an order changing the name of said minor child

from _____

to _____

Verification

I/We hereby certify that all statements made in the foregoing Petition to Change Name of Minor Child are true to the best of my/our knowledge and belief. I/We am/are aware that perjury and willful false statements will subject me/us to punishment under the law.

_____   _____
Petitioner's Signature   Date

_____   _____
Address   Telephone

Subscribed and sworn to before me on this _____ day of_____, 19_____.

_____
Notary

Consent to Name Change

Petitioner's Name(s) _____   Court _____

_____   Docket No. _____

In re: Name Change of Minor Child

From: _____

To: _____

I hereby declare the following:

1. My name is _____ and I currently reside at the following address :

_____

2. I consent to the Petition to Change Name of Minor Child

from _____

to _____.

3. I understand the legal effect of such a change of name, and I have no objections to this court issuing an order to effect said change of name.

Verification

I hereby certify that all statements made in the foregoing Consent to Name Change are true to the best of my knowledge and belief. I am aware that perjury and willful false statements will subject me to punishment under the law.

_____   _____
Signature   Date

Subscribed and sworn to before me on this _____ day of _____,19____.

_____
Notary

16 Being Successful in Small Claims Court

Knowing about Small Claims Court

Small claims courts have been set up in most states to provide an easy procedure for you to assert legal rights. These small claims courts are special courts which are designed to provide speedy, informal, and inexpensive adjudication of small amounts. Small claims court is an ideal forum for self-representation. Legal representation by an attorney is not required and usually not needed. With sufficient documentation, witness testimony, or other proof, and a general understanding of the relevant law, you can adequately present or defend your own case.

Small claims courts typically have limits on the types and dollar amounts of cases which can be decided. Cases in small claims court are normally restricted to the collection of small debts, accounts, property damages, damages for physical injuries, security deposits, damages for breach of contract, or other monetary damages. These courts usually cannot be used to bring actions for libel, slander, professional malpractice, assigned claims, punitive damages meant as punishment or a penalty for wrongful conduct, injunctions to stop some activity or conduct, or other complex issues.

Small claims courts tend to be limited to cases involving claims not exceeding amounts ranging from about $1000 to $5000. In many small claims courts you can waive the amount of your claim which exceeds the dollar limitation and still bring your case in small claims court. However, you cannot recover more than the dollar limit.

Your costs for bringing a case in small claims court, without an attorney, will usually consist of only the basic filing fee. The filing fees generally range from about $10 to $35, depending on your particular jurisdiction. Check with your small claims court for specific filing fees, dollar limits on your claim, and other requirements.

Typical attorney fees for cases in small claims court range from about $200 to $1000, depending on location and the complexity of the case.

Cases in small claims court are civil actions in which one party is suing another party to recover money. If you filed the lawsuit, you are the plaintiff. You have the burden of proving the basis for your claim and the amount of your damages. On the other hand, the defendant is the party against whom the case is brought, and who is summoned to court to defend against the lawsuit.

Should You Go to Court?

Going to court should be your last resort in resolving claims and other disputes. This is because litigation can involve a lot of time, money, and effort. Also, most regular court schedules are overcrowded, and it could take 2-3 years or longer before your civil action comes to trial.

You should always look for ways to settle your case out of court, if possible. Try to negotiate a reasonable settlement with the defendant. Consider alternative dispute resolution procedures, such as arbitration or mediation where an independent third party hears both sides and decides the case out of court. Private and governmental consumer agencies can be helpful in settling disputes over goods and services. Also, the Better Business Bureau in your area may offer a consumer arbitration program for settling consumer business disputes.

Before you file suit in court, be aware that the law may not provide a remedy for every wrong or harm done to you. For example, if your neighbor's tree fell on your car you may not have a claim against your neighbor, unless you can show that he or she was negligent. Likewise, if someone broke a promise to do something for you, he or she would not be liable to you unless you have an enforceable contract. Usually, before you can recover in court, you must show that you have suffered some damages and that the defendant legally caused those damages through intent, negligence, or breach of contract.

The law of negligence protects people from the unreasonable risks of harm caused by others. A person is considered negligent when he or she fails to conduct him- or herself as the average reasonable person would have done under the circumstances. You must generally prove all of the following elements to win a case in court based on negligence:

- violation of a recognized duty of care by the defendant,
- actual and legal cause of the resulting harm by the defendant, and
- damages or injuries suffered by you which are recognizable and measurable.

The violation of the duty of care can result from something that the defendant did or something that he or she failed to do. The required duty of care is always that which the average reasonable person would have

exercised under the circumstances. The standard of care for adults is that of a reasonable adult. The standard of care required of children is that of a child of similar age, intelligence, and experience. If a person has special professional skills, such as a lawyer or doctor, he or she is held to the standard of care normally exercised by members of that profession or trade. If a professional has violated his or her duty of care, it is commonly called malpractice. Malpractice cases can be very complex and usually require expert testimony from members of the profession to prove the required standard of care.

To win a negligence lawsuit, you must prove that the defendant's conduct was the actual and legal cause of your harm. You must typically show that you would not have been injured but for the defendant's act. You must also show that the harm caused to you was reasonably foreseeable by the defendant.

The damages that you can normally recover for negligence in small claims court can be medical expenses, lost wages, and property damage. In a regular lawsuit, not brought in small claims court, you may also recover for pain and suffering and disabilities which will prevent or diminish your future ability to work.

Your conduct is also important if you sue someone for negligence. In many states you will not be able to recover if you have been contributorily negligent in causing your own harm or if you have assumed the risks of any harm suffered. Other states may allow a partial recovery based on the percentage of the defendant's negligence. For example, if the defendant is 60 percent negligent in causing your harm, you may only recover 60 percent of your damages.

You can bring an action in small claims court for breach of contract. You must be able to show the existence of a valid contract by a written document or testimony. A valid contract requires that there be an offer, acceptance, and sufficient consideration. An offer is a proposal to enter into a contract with someone. An acceptance is the indication by the other party that he or she agrees to the terms of your offer. A contract is formed once the offer has been accepted.

A true contract contains at least one promise that is exchanged for something. The promise can be exchanged for another promise, for some act, or for a forbearance from exercising a legal right. The exchange of promises or other things in a contract is consideration. The consideration must have some value in order to be legally sufficient. In other words, if you promise or give nothing under a contract, you cannot enforce the contract because it lacks consideration.

All of your contracts should be in writing and signed by you and the other contracting party. This makes it easy to prove both the existence of a contract and the specific terms and conditions thereof. Certain contracts are generally required to be in writing to be enforceable. These typically include the following:

- A contract for the sale, lease, or mortgage of any interest in land;
- A contract to answer for the debts of another, such as a cosigner or guarantor;
- A contract that, by its terms, cannot be performed within one year after the date of its making;
- A contract for the sale of goods having a price of $500 or more; and
- A contract for the sale of stock and other securities.

Minor children and mentally incompetent persons normally do not have the capacity to enter into a binding contract. A minor can void any contract that he or she has entered into, except contracts for necessities such as food, clothing, or shelter. If a person has been declared mentally incompetent by a court, then any contract that person enters into is completely void. For a person who is mentally incompetent but who has not been so declared by a court, his or her contracts can be voided if he or she so de-sires. With these points in mind, always try to find out as much as possible about the legal capacity of the other party before you enter into a contract.

When you sue someone for breach of contract, you can normally recover any damages caused by the breach. You may also be able to recover any money or property you may have given under the contract or the value of any services you may have rendered. It is also common to request that the court award you any court costs, expenses and legal fees you have incurred in bringing the lawsuit.

You should only go to court if your dispute cannot be settled outside of court, and only if you have a valid claim or cause of action. Courts do not welcome frivolous lawsuits. Some courts may even impose penalties on you for bringing a trivial and groundless lawsuit.

Bringing Your Case in Court
Your court case starts by you filing a civil complaint with the proper court. Most small claims courts have preprinted forms for filing your complaint. These forms vary from state to state, but typically require you to fill out your name and address, the defendant's name and address, a statement giving the basis of your claim, and the amount being sued for. The complaint form is signed by you and may require a verification or declaration under penalty of perjury. Check with the court clerk at your small claims court or other appropriate court for filing forms, procedures, fees and other requirements.

A sample civil complaint form is provided at the end of this chapter. This form should be adaptable for use in most states. You complete the sample form with your name, as the plaintiff, and the name of the defendant. Identify the court and the nature of your complaint, such as "Complaint for Breach of Contract" or the like. The complaint includes declarations as to your address, the defendant's address, and facts to make out your cause of action. The complaint concludes with a request for a judgement against the defendant, a verification and your signature.

Your complaint should give the nature of the defendant's identity, such as an individual, partnership or corporation. If you are suing more than one defendant, be sure to separately identify each one. When suing a business, the defendants should be the business owners, whether a proprietor or partners. Corporations should be sued in their legal names. It is important in many states that you include the correct and exact name of the defendant or any judgment that you win may be defective.

You must file your case in court before the statute of limitation has run. Check the specific time periods for your state at the court clerk's office or your local library. The statute of limitation for contract actions is typically four years from the date of breach or default. Negligence cases normally have a two-year statute of limitation.

After your complaint is filed with the court, it is typically served on the defendant by certified mail or personal service. The defendant is given a specified time period (usually 2-4 weeks) to file an answer to your complaint. The court then sets a date for a hearing to decide the case.

It is important that you prepare your case using good documentary evidence and witnesses, if possible. The presentation of your case in small claims court is very informal. Nevertheless, you should do your best to present a strong and logical case. Bring copies of any necessary documents to court with you, such as contracts, police reports, medical bills, and receipts for repairs and damages. Ask witnesses to accompany you to court to give their testimony. However, if they cannot appear, have them prepare and sign affidavits which contain their testimony. Photographs can also be useful to show the extent of damages or the existence of any unsafe conditions. Your own testimony is also extremely important in proving your case in court.

Likewise, if you are a defendant in a lawsuit, you should adequately prepare to defend against the lawsuit. In many states you must file a written answer to the complaint before the case goes to trial. You may deny any fault or liability on your part, or challenge the amount of the plaintiff's claim. You can also counterclaim against the plaintiff for any loss or damages to you caused by the plaintiff.

Using Affidavits to Help Prove Your Case

In some cases you will be unable to get important witnesses to attend your trial and give testimony. Even if you were to subpoena a witness, he or she might be unfriendly and unwilling to testify favorably for your case. Although it is usually better to have witnesses appear in person to testify, you may be able to use an affidavit when the witness will be unavailable or unwilling to appear in court.

An affidavit is a sworn statement used to verify or prove statements of facts or allegations. The affidavit is written and signed by the witness or declarant under oath before an officer authorized to administer oaths. These officers are typically judges, magistrates, or notaries. Affidavits may be useful in court and out of court for various limited purposes, such as evidence, proof of service, and proof of the existence of a witness. Because affidavits constitute hearsay, they are not normally admissible in regular civil cases as proof of the statements contained therein. However, formal rules of evidence may not be strictly followed in small claims courts. So, affidavits may be extremely helpful in proving your case in small claims court.

Anyone who is competent to testify in court and who has knowledge of the facts can make an affidavit. A legally sufficient affidavit must include:

- the declarant's name and address,
- statement that the declarant was duly sworn under oath,

- statement of facts,
- signature of declarant and date,
- statement that the affidavit was made before a duly authorized officer, and
- signature and title of the officer.

A sample affidavit form is provided at the end of this chapter. You should check the specific requirements for affidavits in your state.

Winning and Collecting a Judgment

Most cases brought in small claims court are lost by the defendant because the defendant failed to show up for the trial or hearing. In such a situation, the plaintiff usually wins a default judgement for everything asked for in the complaint. If the plaintiff fails to appear at trial, the court may decide the case based on the defendant's evidence or dismiss the case all together. If both the plaintiff and defendant show up for trial and present their cases, a magistrate, judge or arbitrator will decide the issues and render a judgement.

Winning a judgement against the defendant in court is merely an announcement that you have won. After winning, you still have to collect on your judgement. The defendant may pay you outright, but more often you have to make efforts to collect your award. The court clerk or judge may tell you what collection procedures you can follow for your state. Typically, you will need to get an order or writ of execution on the judgement from the court. This is then given to your sheriff, who will attach and sell property of the defendant to satisfy your judgement. You must normally locate the defendant's property and assets and provide this information to your sheriff. If the defendant has no property or assets, or these can not be located, you may not be able to collect your judgement now. However, judgements are usually good for a period of five years or longer and they can be renewed thereafter.

Checklist for Bringing a Civil Case in Court

❏ Do you have a valid claim? (i.e. Have you suffered any damages? Was someone else at fault?)

❏ Obtain names and addresses of all parties who have caused you damages.

❏ Notify each party of your claim and try to settle the matter out of court, if possible.

❏ Check statute of limitation in your state for your case.

❏ Check with your court clerk for filing procedures, filing fees, and other requirements.

❏ Prepare a civil complaint against the defendant(s). Specifically set forth the facts and basis for your claim. Attach any relevant t documents, such as contracts, receipts, affidavits, etc. Sign and verify your complaint.

❏ File your complaint with the appropriate court. Obtain a docket number for your case from the court clerk.

❏ Serve a copy of the complaint on defendant(s).

❏ Prepare your case for trial by organizing your presentation, gathering witnesses, and obtaining any other necessary documents or information.

❏ Attend the trial or hearing and present your case.

❏ Receive a judgement from the court deciding your case.

❏ If the judgement is favorable to you, collect on the judgement from the defendant(s). If you are unable to collect from the defendant(s), obtain an order or writ of execution on the judgement, locate the property or assets of the defendant(s), and have your sheriff execute the judgement.

❏ If the judgement is adverse to you, consider filing an appeal if you believe the court has made errors of law. Check with your court clerk for the procedures and requirements for filing an appeal.

❏ Obtain legal counsel if your case involves difficult or complex issues.

Civil Complaint

_____,
Plaintiff

v.

_____
Defendant

Court _____

Docket No. _____

Civil Action _____

Complaint For_____

Plaintiff hereby declares the following:

1. Plaintiff resides at the following address _____

2. Defendant is: (check one)

    ❑ **a)** An individual residing at the following address _____

    ❑ **b)** An individual doing business as _____,
            located at the following address _____

    ❑ **c)** A corporation having a place of business at the following address:

            _____

    ❑ **d)** Other:

3. Plaintiff has a claim against the defendant based on the following:

4. Plaintiff has suffered damages caused by the defendant in the total amount of _____ Dollars ($_____). These damages are specifically listed and described below:

5. Other declarations:

6. Wherefore, Plaintiff requests the court to issue a judgement for Plaintiff and against Defendant in the amount of _____ _____ Dollars ($_____), plus costs, and such further relief as the court deems equitable and just.

Verification

I hereby certify that all statements made in the foregoing civil complaint are true to the best of my knowledge and belief. I am aware that willful false statements can subject me to punishment under the law.

_____   _____
Plaintiff's signature   Date

_____   _____
Plaintiff's Address   Plaintiff's Telephone

Subscribed and sworn to before me on this _____ day of _____ 19_____.

_____
Notary

Affidavit

I, _____,

being of full age, and being duly sworn according to law, upon my oath, state the following:

1. My current residence is as follows:

2. I declare that:

I do solemnly swear and certify that the foregoing statements are true to the best of my knowledge and belief. I am aware that willful false statements can subject me to punishment under the law.

_____   _____
Signature   Date

_____   _____
Address   Telephone

Subscribed and sworn to before me on this _____ day of _____ 19_____.

_____
Notary

Chapter

17 Using Releases to Settle Legal Claims

Releasing Someone from a Claim

It is common to settle legal disputes without resorting to court action. In many cases, the party at fault pays an agreed sum and receives in exchange a release. A release is an agreement by which you discharge or excuse someone from liability arising out of some specific set of circumstances. When you execute and deliver a release to someone, you give up your right to pursue the released claim against that person.

Releases can be used to settle any existing claim or right. This includes rights to enforce a contract, causes of action for negligence, liens, accounts, debts, covenants, rents, and many other legal rights or remedies. In many states, a release which discharges someone from liability for his or her future negligence may be invalid. In other states, the language of the release must be clear and specific to discharge liability for future injuries and disabilities.

A release is like a contract and should be in writing and supported by valuable consideration. The consideration may be payment of money or performance of some act by the party being released. Your release and waiver of your claim is sufficient consideration on your part. To be effective, your release must be signed by you and delivered to the party being released.

It is common for you to sign a release in settling accident and insurance claims. Settling these claims can be relatively simple and easy for you to handle without hiring a lawyer. The following steps may be helpful to you in settling an accident or insurance claim.

If you are involved in an automobile or other accident, gather as many details and facts as possible. Get the owner's name, address, and any insurance information of any other vehicles involved. Get names, addresses, and telephone numbers of all witnesses and of the drivers and passengers of any automobiles involved. If the police were called, ask for a copy of any police reports regarding the accident. Draw a sketch of the scene indicating where the accident happened. Take photographs of the accident if possible.

Whether you think you are injured or not, go to a doctor. You may be injured and not know it. The doctor or hospital visit will confirm any injuries and produce important medical records. Regular visits to the doctor may be necessary if your injuries are severe.

You should write a letter to your insurance company and the insurance companies of any parties at fault. Inform the insurance companies of the date, place, and other details of the accident. The insurance companies will normally give you a claim number and the name of an insurance adjuster who will be handling your case.

Gather all of your doctor bills, medical expenses and other expenses associated with your injury. Ask your doctor for a typewritten medical report signed by the doctor. Send copies (keep originals for your file) of these documents to the insurance company of the party at fault, along with a letter demanding a certain amount as settlement of the claim. Be sure to include in your claim an amount for lost wages and pain and suffering.

You seek to negotiate a settlement with the insurance company which is fair and reasonable to you. If a settlement is reached, you will be asked to sign a release in exchange for payment of the settlement amount. You should consult an attorney if your claim involves complex issues. Attorneys typically handle personal injury cases on a contingency basis for one-third to one-half of any recovery.

A sample release form is provided at the end of this chapter. The release should include the name and address of the party being released (i.e. debtor or defendant). It should also include the name and address of the party giving the release (i.e. claimant). A description of the claim being released should also be included, as well as a description of the consideration to be paid or exchanged for the release. The release should settle all claims arising from the dispute, transaction, or situation, and it should be binding on all parties and their heirs and assigns. Include any additional terms and conditions that may be applicable. The release must be signed by the party giving the release and should be signed by the released party to indicate his or her acceptance.

Release

1. This Release is made and delivered on this _____ day of _____ 19_____ by and between
   _____(Claimant's name)
   _____(Claimant's address)
   and_____(Debtor's name)
   _____(Debtor's address).

2. Claimant hereby discharges and releases Debtor from all claims, actions, damages, and liabilities whatsoever, including those currently known and those which may arise in the future, resulting from or arising out of the following transactions, events, or circumstances:

3. In consideration for this Release, Debtor hereby agrees to pay to Claimant the sum of _____
   _____Dollars ($_____) or to perform the following:

   The above consideration shall be paid or given by Debtor on or before the _____ day of _____ 19___.

4. This Release shall be binding on and inure to the benefit of Claimant and Debtor and their respective heirs, assigns, successors, and legal representatives.

5. Other Terms and Conditions:

6. This Release shall be governed by the laws of the State of _____. This Release is executed and delivered voluntarily as a fair settlement of the foregoing claim(s).

Claimant and Debtor, intending to be legally bound, have signed this Release on the date first indicated above.

_____
Claimant's signature

_____
Debtor's signature

Subscribed and sworn to before me on this _____ day of _____19____.

_____
Notary

18 Patenting and Marketing Your Ideas and Inventions

What Do You Do with Your Ideas?

Innovative ideas are essential to business progress. It is very difficult, however, for innovators to get the kind of financial and management support they need to realize their ideas. This chapter provides some basic information on patenting and marketing your ideas and inventions. Much of this information was made available by the U.S. Small Business Administration and the U.S. Patent and Trademark Office.

Have you had an idea for an invention or an innovative way of doing something that will boost productivity, put more people to work, and make lots of money for you and anyone who backs you? As you have probably heard, you are the kind of person your country needs to compete in world markets and maintain its standard of living. You are the cutting edge of the future.

The chance that you are the first to come up with a particular invention are usually small. And, even if you are the first to come up with the better mouse trap, nobody is going to beat a path to your door.

New product failure rates are estimated to be between fifty and eighty percent. Even for major companies with millions of dollars to spend on research and development, market research, and product advertising — and which aleady have well-established distribution systems, less than ten percent of new product ideas make it past serious review. From these only one or two percent will emerge as a successful new product.

Although coming up with what you think is a great idea is the biggest step, it's still only the first one. Many things remain to be done before you can expect to realize the first dollar from your invention or idea. You should be prepared for the unhappy discovery that the idea or invention may ultimately fail.

You need to find out whether your idea is original or someone else has already come up with it? There are lots of places to look to find out. If your idea is for a consumer product, check stores and catalogs. Check trade associations and trade publications in the field into which your invention or idea fits and visit relevant trade shows. If what you have come up with is an invention or an idea that can be patented, you should eventually make a patent search and file a patent application.

The first thought many inventors have is to take their ideas to a big national company. Unfortunately, most major companies are not interested in ideas from outsiders. If you so approach a company or anyone else about your idea, try to get them to sign a nondisclosure agreement. The nondisclosure agreement obligates the other party to maintain your idea in confidence and not use or disclose it without your permission. If the other party refuses to sign a nondisclosure agreement, it is best to have your invention patented before you disclose it. You should nevertheless make it clear in writing to the other party that any disclosures that you make are in confidence and that you expect compensation if your invention is ever used.

You may be able to produce some items yourself, working out of your home and selling by mail order. This method can be a good way to get started. If you can start (or already have) your own company, you will be better off. It may be easier to sell a company than an idea or patent, even if the company is losing money.

Between the extremes of starting your own company or having a big business buy you out is taking your idea to small and medium-sized businesses. Such firms may be happy to produce an item that sells in amounts too small to interest large companies. Smaller firms may lack marketing and distribution expertise, but again your major problem is simply finding one that is able and interested in trying to make your idea a reality.

Can You Protect Your Idea?

Once you have looked at issues such as originality, production and distribution, and marketability, it's time to consider protecting your idea. If you do have a patentable idea, look into trying to protect it under the patent laws.

To document your invention, get a close friend (who understands your invention) to sign his or her name on a dated diagram or written description of the invention. You can also file a "disclosure document" with the U.S. Patent Office. Taking one of these measures will provide evidence of the time you came up with your invention in case of a dispute with other inventors over who conceived it first. Sending yourself a registered letter describing the invention is useless as evidence. Filing a disclosure document with the U.S. Patent Office does not give you any patent protection but only provides evidence of your invention.

Make a patent search to see whether or not the invention has already been pat-

ented. You can make a search yourself at the Patent and Trademark Office, Crystal Plaza, Arlington, Virginia. The staff at the Patent Office will give you some help in conducting patent searches and using Patent Office faciliites. If your invention is complex or involves complicated issues, you may need the help of a patent agent or patent attorney.

If the invention has not already been patented, you can prepare a patent application and file it with the U.S. Patent and Trademark Office. Specific information on preparing and filing a simple U.S. patent application is presented later in this chapter.

Where Can You Go for Help?

While you probably still have to invest considerable time, money, and effort your invention, you can get help from the following sources:

- **Patent Attorneys and Agents.** Attorneys and agents can help you make a patent search and file a patent application, if you can't do them yourself. The U.S. Patent Office has geographical and alphabetical listings of such people, but doesn't make recommendations or assume any responsibility for your selection from its lists. You can also find attorneys and agents by looking in the classified section of your telephone directory under "Patent Attorneys." Typical attorney's fees for preparing and filing a simple patent application range from about $1000 to $3000.

- **Invention Promotion Firms.** Also likely to be listed in the "Patents" section of the telephone directory are firms that offer — for a fee — to take on the whole job of protecting and promoting your idea. Caution is necessary in dealing with such promoters. They typically charge fees ranging from $2000 to $5000 and may not have a proven track record.

If you elect to use an idea promotion firm, choose one that:

(1) can provide you with solid evidence of their track record — not just a few flashy success stories, but verifiable statistics on the number of clients they've had and the number who have actually made money.

(2) don't collect the entire fee in advance.

(3) will provide you with samples of their promotional materials and lists of companies to whom they have sent it. Then check with those companies yourself. Check the promotion firm's reputation with the local Better Business Bureau, Chamber of Commerce, a patent attorney, local inventors or innovators club, or with former clients of the firm.

- **Invention Brokers.** Brokers work for a portion of the profits from an invention. They may help inventors raise capital and form companies to produce and market their inventions. They often provide sophisticated management advice. In general, you can expect these brokers to be interested in more complex technology with fairly large sales potential.

- **University Invention/Entrepreneurial Centers.** These centers, some funded by the National Science Foundation, may provide some help for inventors and innovators. The University of Oregon's Experimental Center for the Advancement of Invention and Innovation, for example, evaluates ideas for a very modest fee.

  The Center does this to help inventors weed out bad ideas so they won't waste further time and money on them. The Center can also identify trouble spots that require special attention in planning the development or commercialization of a potential new product. If an idea looks like it has merit and is commercially feasible, the Center tries to link the inventor with established companies or refer him or her to sources of funds. Similar programs may be available at other colleges and universities.

- **The Small Business Administration.** The SBA's Small Business Institutes (SBI's) are located at more than several hundred colleges and universities around the country. While currently few SBI schools can provide much help with the technical research and development aspects of innovations, they may be able to provide the market research, feasibility analysis, and business planning assistance necessary to make an invention successful.

  SBA field offices (see your local telephone directory under "U.S. Government") can provide you with information about the SBI program. You may find other management assistance programs offered at the field offices which may be of help in developing your idea as well. Publications containing information on patenting and marketing inventions are available by writing to Small Business Administration, 1441 L St., N.W., Washington, D.C. 20416.

- **National Bureau of Standards.** The Office of Energy- Related Inventions in the U.S. Department of Commerce's National Bureau of Standards sometimes evaluates non-nuclear energy-related inventions and ideas for devices, materials, and procedures without charge. If the office finds that the invention or idea has merit, it can recommend further study by the Department of Energy which may provide support for the invention if it shows promise. This process can take from nine months to a year.

- **Inventor's Clubs/Associations/Societies.** You may have such clubs in your locality. Talking with other inventors is probably the most helpful thing you can do. Find someone who has been through the entire routine of patents, applied research and development, and stages of financing. It doesn't matter if the end result was a financial success or failure. Getting the nuts and bolts of the process can be very important.

What Is a Patent?

A patent is a grant by the U.S. government to an inventor of the right to exclude others from making, using, or selling his or her invention in the United States, its territories, and possessions. A patent is issued to the inventor by the U.S. Patent and Trademark Office, and can be effective for a period of seventeen years depending upon the payment of maintenance fees.

The essential nature of a patent is the right to exclude. The patent does not grant the right to make, use, or sell the invention, but only grants the right to exclude others from doing this. Since the patent does not grant the right to make, use, or sell the invention, the patentee's own right to do so is dependent upon the rights of others and whatever general laws might be applicable. A patentee may not sell an article, the sale of which is forbidden by law, merely because he or she has obtained a patent. Neither may a patentee make, use, or sell his or her own invention if doing so would infringe the prior rights of others.

Since the essence of the right granted by a patent is the right to exclude others from commercial use of the invention, the patentee is the only one who may make, use, or sell his or her invention. Others may not do so without authorization from the patentee. Thus a patent owner may choose to manufacture and sell the invention or may license others to do so.

Some people occasionally confuse patents, copyrights, and trademarks. Although there may be some resemblance in these three kinds of intellectual property, they serve different functions. Copyright protects the writings and artistic works of an author or artist against copying. Literary, dramatic, musical, and artistic works are included within the protection of the copyright law, which protects only the form of expression rather than the subject matter of the writing. A trademark relates to any word, name, symbol or device that is used in trade with goods or services to indicate the source or origin of the goods and to distinguish them from the goods of others. Trademark rights would prevent others from using a confusingly similar mark, but would not prevent others from making the same goods or from selling them under a nonconfusing mark.

The patent law specifies the general field of subject matter that can be patented and the conditions under which a patent may be obtained. Any person who invents or discovers any new and useful process, machine, article of manufacture, or composition of matter, or any new and useful improvements thereof, may obtain a patent, subject to the conditions and requirements of the law. A process means a process, method, or set of steps. A machine is a device or equipment for performing physical functions. Articles of manufacture refer to goods and products that are made, and includes all manufactured articles. Composition of matter relates to chemical compositions, and may include mixtures of ingredients as well as new chemical compounds. These classes of subject matter taken together include practically everything that is made by man and the processes for making them.

The patent law requires that an invention must be useful. This means that the invention must have a useful purpose and must be operative; that is, the invention must operate to perform its intended purpose. An invention may be useful, although it is destructive. For example, a gun or explosive may be patentable subject matter, although its primary purpose is to kill or destroy.

Certain inventions are held not to be patentable because of policy reasons. Alleged inventions of perpetual motion machines are not patentable. Methods of doing business and printed matter cannot be patented. Inventions useful solely in the utilization of special nuclear material or atomic energy for atomic weapons are excluded from patent protection by the Atomic Energy Act. A patent cannot be obtained upon a mere idea or suggestion; rather, a complete description and reduction to practice of the invention is required.

In addition to the utility patent discussed above, a design or plant patent may be obtained. A design patent may be granted to any person who has invented any new, original, and ornamental design for an article of manufacture. The design patent is effective for fourteen years and protects only the appearance of an article but not its structure or utility features. A plant patent may be granted to anyone who has invented or discovered and asexually reproduced any distinct and new variety of plant. This includes cultivated sports, mutants, hybrids, and newly found seedlings, other than a plant found in an uncultivated state or a tuber-propagated plant such as the Irish potato.

Conception and Reduction to Practice

A bare idea or concept, without more, is not patentable. In order for a discovery to be a patentable invention, there must be a demonstration of the concept. Invention equals conception plus reduction to practice.

"Conception" means the mental formulation of the invention in sufficient detail that a person, familiar with the subject matter to which the invention relates, could make and use the invention.

Reduction to practice generally involves making or constructing the invention (i.e., preparing a compound or composition) and testing it to demonstrate that it is useful for its conceived purpose.

What Is a Patentable Invention?

In order for an invention to be patentable in the U.S., the invention must be:

(1) *new* (novel)
(2) *useful*
(3) *unobvious*

To be new is required by the patent statute, which states that an invention cannot be patented if:

(a) The invention was known or used by others in this country, or patented or described in a printed publication in this or a foreign country, before the invention thereof by the applicant for patent, or

(b) The invention was patented or described in a printed publication in this or a foreign country, or in public use or on sale in this country, more than one year prior to the application for patent in the United States...

If the invention has been described in a printed publication anywhere in the world, or if it has been in public use or on sale in this country before the date that you made your invention, a patent cannot be obtained. Also, a valid patent cannot be obtained if the invention has been described in a printed publication anywhere, or has been in public use or on sale in this country for one year or more. In this connection, it is immaterial when the invention was made, or whether the printed publication or public use was by you or by someone else. If you described the invention in a printed publication or used the invention publicly, or placed it on sale, you must apply for a patent before one year has gone by, otherwise any right to a patent will be lost.

The usefulness test is easily met if you can show that your invention operates to perform some function.

Typically the most difficult hurdle to overcome in establishing patentability is whether the invention is obvious. A patent may not be obtained even though the invention is not identically disclosed or described in the "prior art" if the differences between the subject matter sought to be patented and the "prior art" are such that the subject matter "as a whole" would have been "obvious" at the time the invention was made to a person having "ordinary skill in the art" to which the subject matter pertains.

Even if the subject matter sought to be patented is not exactly shown by the prior art, and involves one or more differences over the most nearly similar thing already known, a patent may still be refused if the differences would be obvious. The subject matter sought to be patented must be sufficiently different from what has been used or described before so that it may be said to amount to invention over the prior art. Small advances that would be obvious to a person having ordinary skill in the art are not considered inventions capable of being patented. For example, the substitution of one material for another, or changes in size, are ordinarily not patentable.

If an "inventor" is merely utilizing the teachings or suggestions of the published literature or prior art to solve a problem and no unexpected results are obtained, it is doubtful that the invention overcomes the obviousness test. The invention must be evaluated on the basis of how it relates to the problem faced, the need for a solution, how the invention differs from the published literature, what features of the invention are not taught or suggested (not predictable) from the published literature, and its prospects of commercial success.

Who May Apply for a Patent?

According to the statute, only the inventor may apply for a patent, with certain exceptions. If a person who is not the inventor should apply for a patent, the patent (if it were obtained) would be void. If the person applying in such a case falsely states that he or she is the inventor, that person would also be subject to criminal penalties. If the inventor is dead, the application may be made by his or her legal representatives, such as the administrator or executor of his or her estate. If the inventor is insane or mentally incompetent, the application for patent may be made by his or her guardian. If an inventor refuses to apply for a patent or cannot be found, a joint inventor or a person having a proprietary interest in the invention may apply on behalf of the missing inventor.

If two or more persons make an invention jointly, they must apply for a patent as joint inventors. A person who makes a fi-nancial contribution is not a joint inventor and cannot be joined in the application as an inventor. It is possible to correct an innocent mistake in erroneously omitting an inventor or in erroneously naming a person as an inventor.

Officers and employees of the Patent and Trademark Office are prohibited by law from applying for a patent or acquiring, directly or indirectly, except by inheritance or bequest, any patent or any right or interest in any patent.

Application for Patent

The application for a patent is made to the Commissioner of Patents and Trademarks, Washington, D.C. 20231, and includes:

- A written document which comprises a specification (description and claims) and an oath or declaration;
- a drawing in those cases in which a drawing is helpful and possible; and
- the required filing fee.

The specification and oath or declaration must be in the English language and must be legibly written or printed in permanent ink on one side of the paper. The Office prefers typewritten papers, 8 to 8 1/2 by 10 1/2 to 13 inches, 1 1/2 spaces or double-spaced, with margins of 1 inch on the left-hand side and at the top. If the papers filed are not correctly, legibly, and clearly written, the Patent and Trademark Office may require typewritten or printed papers.

The application for patent can be accepted and assigned a serial number and filing date even if the filing fee and oath/declaration is filed late. The Patent Office will notify you of any deficiencies in the papers filed and will normally give you two months to correct these deficiencies.

It is desirable that all parts of the complete application be filed with the Patent and Trademark Office together; otherwise each part must be signed and accompanied by a letter accurately and clearly connecting it with the other parts of the application.

All applications are numbered consecutively and the applicant is given a filing receipt with the serial number and filing date of the application. The filing date is the date on which a specification (including claims) and any required drawings are received in the Patent and Trademark Office; or the date on which the last part completing such papers are received in the case of a previously incomplete or defective application.

Oath or Declaration and Signature: The oath or declaration of the applicant is required by statute. The inventor must make an oath or declaration that he or she believes himself or herself to be the original and first inventor of the subject matter of the application as well as other allegations required by the statute or the Patent and Trademark Office rules. The oath must be sworn to by the inventor before a notary public or other officer authorized to administer oaths. A declaration may be used in place of an oath. This is a written statement containing the necessary allegations which is signed by the applicant. A sample Declaration for Patent Application form is provided at the end of this chapter.

The application oath or declaration must be signed by the inventor in person, or by the person entitled by law to make application on the inventor's behalf. A full first or middle name for each inventor without abbreviation and a middle or first initial, if any, is required. The post-office address of the inventor is also required.

The papers in a complete application will not be returned for any purpose whatever, nor will the filing fee be returned. If applicants have not preserved copies of the papers, the Office may furnish copies at a cost.

Filing Fees: The filing fee for an application, except in design and plant cases, consists of a basic fee and additional fees. The basic filing fee at the time of this printing is $630 and entitles the applicant to present 20 claims, including not more than 3 in independent form (not dependent on another claim). An additional fee of $60 is required for each claim in independent form that is in excess of 3, and an additional fee of $20 is required for each claim (whether independent or dependent) that is in excess of a total of 20 claims. If the application contains multiple dependent claims which depend on two or more claims, $200 per application is also required. Check with the U.S. Patent and Trademark Office for any changes in the fee schedules.

When the owner of the invention is a small entity the filing fees are reduced by half if a declaration of small entity status is filed. A small entity is an independent inventor, non-profit organization or a small business having 500 employees or less as defined by the Small Business Administration. A sample Declaration Claiming Small Entity Status Form is provided at the end of this chapter.

Specification: The specification must include a written description of the invention and of the manner and process of making and using it. It is required to be in such full, clear, concise, and exact terms as to enable any person skilled in the art to which the invention pertains, or with which it is most nearly connected, to make and use the same.

The specification must set forth the precise invention for which a patent is sought, in such manner as to distinguish it from other inventions and from what is old. It must describe completely a specific embodiment of the process, machine, article of manufacture, composition of matter, or improvements invented, and should explain the mode of operation or principle whenever applicable. The best mode contemplated by you to carry out your invention must be set forth.

The specification must conclude with one or more claims particularly pointing out and distinctly claiming the subject matter which you regard as your invention. The claims are brief descriptions of the subject matter of the invention, eliminating unnecessary details and reciting all essential features necessary to distinguish the invention from what is old. Novelty and patentability are judged by the claims, and, when a patent is granted, questions of infringement are judged by the courts on the basis of the claims.

The following order should be observed in framing the specification:

(a) Title of the invention.
(b) Cross-references to related applications, if any.
(c) Background of the invention, including a description of the prior art.
(d) Brief summary of the invention.
(e) Brief description of the several views of the drawings, if there are drawings.
(f) Detailed description of the invention.
(g) Claim or claims.
(h) Abstract of the disclosure.
(i) Drawing, if any.

(a) Title of Invention

The considerations governing the choice of a title for the invention or application are as follows: The title of the invention, which should be as short and specific as possible, should appear as a heading on the first page of the specification, if it does not otherwise appear at the beginning of the application. The title should be brief but technically accurate and descriptive.

(b) Cross References to Related Applications

This is merely a statement identifying patent applications, if any, which are part of a chain of applications pending in the U.S. Patent and Trademark Office. A continuation, continuation-in-part, or a divisional application may claim the benefit of the filing date of an earlier U.S. or foreign patent application.

(c) Background of the Invention

This section generally includes a description of the field of the invention and a description of the prior art. The description of the prior art should state the prior art known to you, including references to specific publications or patents. The problems involved in the prior art, which are solved by your invention, should also be indicated. You are required to disclose to the U.S. Patent and Trademark Office any material prior art of which you are aware.

(d) Summary of the Invention

A brief summary of the invention indicating its nature and substance, which may include a statement of the object of the invention, should precede the detailed description. Such summary should be commensurate with the invention as claimed and any object recited should be that of the invention as claimed.

(e) Description of the Drawings

The purpose of the description of the drawings is to relate the drawings to the object which they are supposed to depict. Drawings are not always required in a patent application, except when they are necessary to understand the invention. Drawings may be used whenever they are helpful in illustrating the invention. The drawing may be in the form of sketches, graphs, photographs, etc.

(f) Detailed Description

A detailed description of the invention includes a complete discussion on how to make and use the invention.

In chemical cases, the description would include a disclosure of the method of making and using the compound, composition, or process, and disclosure of other suitable embodiments of the invention. Thus in chemical compound cases, this section of the application should include a description and listing of suitable starting materials, the method of their preparation (if they are not otherwise available), the method of converting the starting materials into the compound, a specific description of the compound itself, and the method of using the compound. If the invention is a composition involving a combination of ingredients, this section should include a detailed description of the composition and a listing of suitable ingredients and proportions thereof. When the invention is a process, the section should include a detailed description of each step, including process conditions, suitable processing apparatus, and suitable materials to be used.

In mechanical cases, this description normally involves identification and description of each of the elements depicted in the drawings, identifying the elements by means of their reference numerals, as well as a description of other alternative embodiments. This also includes a description of the manner in which the device works, showing the functional relationship between the elements defined in the drawings.

The specification must also describe the "best mode" contemplated by you, at the time of filing, to carry out your invention. The purpose of this requirement is to restrain inventors from applying for patents while at the same time concealing from the public preferred embodiments of their inventions which they have in fact conceived.

The best mode requirement is satisfied by disclosing at least one working embodiment which corresponds to the best mode of the invention contemplated by the inventor at the time of filing. However, the invention should be claimed more broadly than a claim covering only one embodiment of the invention. Failure to disclose the best mode can invalidate the patent.

The purpose of "working examples," like the purpose of the rest of the specification, is to describe the invention and the method of making and using it. The working examples are more detailed than the broader descriptions in the specification, and provide the most detailed features of the invention. The working examples are actual experiments carried out by the inventor to demonstrate the invention. Although a U.S. patent may be obtained without any working examples, it is always advantageous to include one or more working examples.

Working examples can dispel doubts as to the operability or utility of the invention particularly in pharmaceutical inventions where utility must be clearly demonstrated. These examples can demonstrate the scope of the various embodiments of the invention. Working examples can also show highly beneficial or surprising results which are useful in showing unobviousness. Working examples, in the form of experimental comparisons with the prior art, are especially useful in showing that the invention is not obvious from the prior art because the invention yields unexpected results.

A question arises as to how detailed the description of a working example should be. The rule is that the example as written must be complete and not be misleading. That is, it should define each step of the embodiment in a manner which would clearly convey to the person skilled in the art what was or should be done, without leaving out important steps or conditions. Results other than those actually obtained under the conditions of the example should not be reported. On the other hand, inconsequential and irrelevant details need not be reported in the examples.

"Paper" or "prophetic" examples may be used in a U.S. patent application. However, these paper examples are not considered as persuasive as working examples, and paper examples may not be sufficient for patent applications in many foreign countries. Paper examples are simply statements by the applicant as to how a working example should be carried out, even though he or she has not actually done so. Paper examples are written in the present or future tense to distinguish them from working examples which are usually written in the past tense.

(g) Patent Claims

The claims are perhaps the most important part of a patent as they define the invention which is protected by the patent. It is the patent claims which are used to determine questions of infringement.

The format of a patent claim is essentially a run-on sentence which may be broken down into a preamble, a transitional phrase and the body of the claim. The preamble generally states the class into which the invention falls (i.e. a composition, method, apparatus, etc.), and may be coupled with a statement of intended use or purpose.

The transitional phrase of a patent claim indicates whether the elements in the body of the claim are closed or are left open to additional elements. The terms "comprising," "including," or "containing" indicate that the claim is open and, therefore, does not exclude additional elements which are not recited in the claim. "Consisting of" or "composed of" characterizes a claim as being closed, and the presence of an additional ingredient would avoid infringement of the claim. If possible, claims should be open to give them broader coverage.

The body of the claim states the essential elements which make up the invention. These elements can be the steps or operations of a process, the component parts of a mechanical device, or the ingredients of a composition of matter. The omission of an element that is essential to the operability of the invention renders the claim invalid. However, elements that are not essential to the invention should not be recited in the claims. Every element of the claim must be adequately described earlier in the specification.

The claims are typically set up in a hierarchy with the broadest claim followed by narrower dependent claims.

(h) Abstract of The Disclosure
The abstract is a short overview of the invention. The purpose of the abstract is to enable the Patent and Trademark Office and the public to determine quickly the nature of the invention and the technical disclosure.

(i) Drawing
The applicant for a patent will usually be required to furnish a drawing of the invention whenever the nature of the case makes it necessary; this drawing must be filed with the application. This requirement may pertain to practically all inventions except compositions of matter or processes, but a drawing may also be useful in the case of many processes.

The drawing must show every feature of the invention specified in the claims and is required by the Office rules to be in a particular form. The Office specifies the size of the sheet on which the drawing is made, the paper, the margins, and other details relating to the making of the drawing (typically, black ink on 8 1/2 by 14 inch white paper). The reason for specifying the standards in detail is that the drawings are printed and published in a uniform style when the patent issues, and the drawings must also be readily understood by persons using the patent descriptions.

Examination of Applications in the U.S. Patent and Trademark Office
Applications filed in the U.S. Patent and Trademark Office and accepted as complete applications are assigned for examination to the respective examining groups having charge of the classes of inventions to which the applications relate. In the examining group, applications are taken up by the examiner to whom they have been assigned in the order in which they have been filed or in accordance with examining procedures established by the Commissioner.

Applications will not be advanced out of turn except as provided by the rules, or upon order of the Commissioner to expedite the business of the Office, or upon a verified showing that, in the opinion of the Commissioner, will justify so advancing it. For example, the application may be advanced if the invention has importance to the government, is useful in protecting the environment or conserving energy, is involved in litigation, or if the applicant is seriously ill.

The examination of the application consists of a study of the application for compliance with the legal requirements. To check for newness of the invention a search is made through the prior art represented by prior United States patents, prior foreign patents that are available in the U.S. Patent and Trademark Office, and such prior literature as may be available.

If prior art that discloses or suggests your invention is found, the patent examiner will send you an office action rejecting your application along with copies of the prior art references. You are generally allowed three to six months to respond to the examiner's rejection by amending your claims or distinguishing your invention from the prior art.

If, on examination of the application, or at a later stage during the reexamination or reconsideration of the application, the patent application is found to be allowable, a notice of allowance will be sent to you. A fee for issuing the patent is due within three months from the date of the notice.

The issue fee for each original patent, except in design and plant cases, is $1,050 at the time of this printing. The amount of the issue fee is reduced by one-half for small entities. If timely payment of the issue fee is not made, the application will be regarded as abandoned (which means that it is forfeited).

A provision is made in the statute by which the Commissioner may accept the fee late on a showing of unintentional or unavoidable delay. The patent issues as soon as possible after the date of payment of the issue fee. The patent is then delivered or mailed on the day of its grant, or as soon thereafter as possible. Maintenance fees are required to keep the patent in force thereafter.

On the date of the grant, the record of the patent in the U.S. Patent and Trademark Office becomes open to the public. Printed copies of the specification and drawing are available on that same date or shortly thereafter.

Infringement of Patents

Infringement of a patent consists of the unauthorized making, using, or selling of the patented invention within the territory of the United States during the term of the patent. If your patent is infringed, you may sue for relief in the appropriate federal court. You may ask the court for an injunction to prevent the continuation of the infringement as well as an award of damages because of the infringement. In such an infringement suit, the defendant may raise the question of the validity of the patent, which is then decided by the court. The defendant may also argue that what he or she is doing does not constitute infringement. Infringement is determined primarily by the language of the claims of the patent. If what the defendant is making does not fall within the language of any of the claims of the patent, he or she generally is not infringing.

Suits for infringement of patents follow the rules of procedure of the federal courts. These are very complex litigations which can be extremely expensive and require legal counsel. From the decision of the district court, there is an appeal to the Court of Appeals for the Federal Circuit. The Supreme Court may thereafter take a case by writ of certiorari at the court's discretion. If the United States government infringes your patent, you have a remedy for damages in the same court. The government may use any patented invention without your permission, but you are entitled to obtain compensation for the use.

If an individual is notified that he or she is infringing a patent or is threatened with suit, that individual may start the suit in a federal court and get a judgment on the matter.

The U.S. Patent and Trademark Office has no jurisdiction over questions relating to infringement of patents. In examining applications for patents, no determination is made as to whether the invention sought to be patented infringes any prior patent. An improvement invention may be patentable, but it might infringe a prior unexpired patent for the invention improved upon (if there is one).

Since the rights granted by a United States patent extend only throughout the territory of the United States and have no effect in a foreign country, an inventor who wishes patent protection in other countries must apply for a patent in each of these countries. Almost every country has its own patent laws, procedures and requirements for applying for patent. The United States has entered into a treaty with most industrialized countries that allows an applicant to file foreign patent applications within one year of the United States filing date and, thus, obtain the benefit of the United States filing date for the foreign applications.

Checklist for
Filing a U.S. Patent Application

❏ Describe your invention in writing, sign and date the description, and have it signed and dated by one or more witnesses who understand the invention.

❏ Do a search of the prior art, including U.S. patents, foreign patents and published articles and books to see if someone else has already made or suggested your invention.

❏ Prepare a typewritten (8 1/2 by 11 inches) patent application according to the required format.

❏ Prepare and sign Transmittal Form for a New Patent Application.

❏ Prepare List of Art Cited by Applicant, if any.

❏ Prepare and sign Declaration for Patent Application.

❏ Prepare and sign Declaration Claiming Small Entity Status, if applicable.

❏ File Transmittal Form, typewritten application, List of Art, Declaration for Patent Application, Declaration Claiming Small Entity Status, and filing fee by

express mail with U.S. Patent and Trademark Office, Washington, D.C. 20231. (Keep a copy for your records.)

❏ Respond to any communications from the U.S. Patent and Trademark Office, including a request for payment of the issue fee, within the time provided by the U.S. Patent and Trademark Office.

❏ Consult a patent attorney if your invention or patent application involves complex or difficult issues.

Transmittal Form for a New Patent Application in the United States Patent and Trademark Office

The Honorable Commissioner of Patents and Trademarks

Dear Sir:

1. Transmitted herewith for filing is a new and original patent application as identified below.

2. Inventor(s) _____

3. Title _____

Enclosed are: (check appropriate boxes)

4. ❑ _____ sheet(s) of ❑ formal   ❑ informal drawing(s).
5. ❑ Declaration For Patent Application.
6. ❑ An assignment of the invention to: _____
7. ❑ Declaration Claiming Small Entity Status.
8. ❑ List of Art Cited by Applicant.
9. ❑ The filing fee is calculated below:

10. ❑ A check in the amount of _____ is enclosed.
11. ❑ Also enclosed:

12. ❑ Address all future communications to _____ (name)

_____ (address)

_____ (telephone)

_____   _____
Signature   Date

Certificate of Express Mailing

I hereby certify that this Transmittal and the documents referred to as enclosed herein are being deposited with the United States Postal Service on _____ in an envelope bearing "Express Mail Post Office to Addressee" Mailing Number _____ addressed to the Commissioner of Patents and Trademarks, Washington, D.C. 20231.

_____
(Typed or printed name of person mailing)

_____
Signature

_____
Date

Declaration Claiming Small Entity Status

Applicant or Patentee _____

Serial or Patent No. _____

Filed or Issued (Date)_____

Title _____

I hereby declare that I am:

    ❑ an inventor of the invention described below.

    ❑ the owner of the small business concern identified below having rights to the invention:

    ❑ an authorized official of the small business concern identified below having rights to the invention:

    Name of Small Business Concern_____

    Address of Small Business Concern_____

I hereby declare that I qualify as ❑ an independent inventor as defined in 37 CFR 1.9(c) or ❑ a small business concern as defined in 37 CFR 1.9 (d) for purposes of paying reduced fees under Section 41(a) and (b) of Title 35, United States Code, to the Patent and Trademark Office with regard to the invention entitled _____ _____ described in

    ❑ the specification filed herewith

    ❑ application serial no. _____, filed _____.

    ❑ patent no. _____, issued _____.

I have not assigned, granted, conveyed, or licensed, and am under no obligation under contract or law to assign, grant, convey, or license, any rights in the invention to any person who could not be classified as an independent inventor under 37 CFR 1.9(c) if that person had made the invention, or to any concern which would not qualify as a small business concern under 37 CFR 1.9(d) or a nonprofit organization under 37 CFR 1.9(e).

    Each person, concern, or organization to which I have assigned, granted, conveyed, or licensed or am under an obligation under contract or law to assign, grant, convey, or license any rights in the invention is listed below:

    ❑ no such person, concern, or organization

    ❑ person, concerns or organizations listed below*

*NOTE: Separate verified statements are required from each named person, concern, or organization having rights to the invention claiming their status as small entities. (37 CFR 1.27)

Full Name_____

Address_____

    ❑ Individual   ❑ Small Business Concern   ❑ Nonprofit Organization

I acknowledge the duty to file, in this application or patent, notification of any change in status resulting in loss of entitlement to small entity status prior to paying, or at the time of paying, the earliest of the issue fee or any maintenance fee due after the date on which status as a small entity is no longer appropriate. (37 CFR 1.28[b]).

    I hereby declare that all statements made herein of my own knowledge are true and that all statements made on information and belief are believed to be true; and further that these statements were made with the knowledge that willful false statements and the like so made are punishable by fine or imprisonment, or both, under Section 1001 of Title 18 of the United States Code, and that such willful false statements may jeopardize the validity of the application, any patent issuing thereon, or any patent to which this verified statement is directed.

_____

Name of Person Signing and Position

_____   _____

Signature   Date

Declaration For Patent Application

As a below named inventor, I hereby declare that:

My residence, post office address and citizenship are as stated below next to my name,

I believe I am the original, first, and sole inventor (if only one name is listed below) or an original, first, and joint inventor (if plural names are listed below) of the subject matter which is claimed and for which a patent is sought on the invention entitled:

the specification of which

(check one) ❏ is attached hereto.

❏ was filed on _____ as

Application Serial No._____

and was amended on _____ (if applicable)

I hereby state that I have reviewed and understand the contents of the above-identified specification, including the claims, as amended by any amendment referred to above.

I acknowledge the duty to disclose information which is material to the examination of this application in accordance with Title 37, Code of Federal Regulations, Section 1.56(a).

I hereby claim foreign priority benefits under Title 35, United States Code, Section 119 of any foreign application(s) for patent or inventor's certificate listed below, and I have also identified below any foreign application for patent or inventor's certificate having a filing date before that of the application on which this foreign priority is claimed:

Prior Foreign Application(s):

Country	Application Number	Date of Filing	Priority Claimed Under 35 U.S.C. 119
_____	_____	_____	❏ YES ❏ NO
_____	_____	_____	❏ YES ❏ NO
_____	_____	_____	❏ YES ❏ NO

I hereby claim the benefit under Title 35, United States Code, Section 120, of any United States application(s) listed below and, insofar as the subject matter of each of the claims of this application is not disclosed in the prior United States application in the manner provided by the first paragraph of Title 35, United States Code, Section 112, I acknowledge the duty to disclose material information as defined in Title 37, Code of Federal Regulations, Section 1.56(a) which occurred between the filing date of the prior application and the national or PCT international filing date of this application:

_____	_____	_____
Application Serial No.	Filing Date	Status (patented, pending, abandoned)
_____	_____	_____
Application Serial No.	Filing Date	Status (patented, pending, abandoned)
_____	_____	_____
Application Serial No.	Filing Date	Status (patented, pending, abandoned)

Address all telephone calls to _____ at telephone number _____.

Address all correspondences to_____ at

the following address:_____.

I hereby declare that all statements made herein of my own knowledge are true and that all statement made on information and belief are believed to be true; and further that these statements were made with the knowledge that willful false statements and the like so made are punishable by fine or imprisonment, or both, under Section 1001 of Title 18 of the United States Code and that such willful false statements may jeopardize the validity of the application or any patent issued thereon.

_____   _____
Inventor's Signature   Date

Full Name of Sole or First Inventor_____

Citizenship _____

Residence _____

Post Office Address _____

_____   _____
Inventor's Signature   Date

Full Name of Second Joint Inventor _____

Citizenship _____

Residence _____

Post Office Address _____

_____   _____
Inventor's Signature   Date

Full Name of Third Joint Inventor_____

Citizenship _____

Residence _____

Post Office Address _____

(Supply similar information and signatures for fourth and subsequent joint inventors.)

List of Art Cited by Applicant (Use several sheets if necessary)

Applicant _____ Serial No. _____ Filing Date _____ Group _____

U.S. Patent Documents

Examiner Iinitial	Document Number	Date	Name	Class	Subclass	Filing Date if appropriate

Foreign Patent Documents

	Document Number	Date	Country	Class	Subclass	Translation Yes No

Other Art (Including Author, Title, Date, Pertinent Pages, Etc.)

Examiner _____ Date Considered _____

*Examiner: Initial if reference considered, whether or not citation is in conformance with MPEP 609: Draw line through citation if not in conformance and not considered. Include copy of this form with next communication to applicant.

Nondisclosure Agreement

1. This Agreement is made on this _____ day of _____19_____ by and between
   _____(Discloser's name)
   _____(Discloser's address)
   and _____(Recipient's name)
   _____(Recipient's address).

   In consideration of the mutual covenants hereinafter set forth and other valuable consideration, the parties hereto agree to the following terms and conditions:

2. Discloser shall disclose to Recipient confidential and proprietary Information of Discloser relating to:

3. Recipient shall use said Information only for the purpose of:

4. Recipient shall maintain said Information in confidence, and shall not disclose said Information to any party, and shall not use said Information in any way whatsoever, except as expressly provided herein. Nothing contained in this Agreement shall be deemed to give Recipient any rights whatsoever in and to said Information.

5. The obligations of confidentiality and nonuse hereunder shall not apply to any information which is or becomes publicly available through no fault of Recipient, or which was already known by Recipient before disclosure by Discloser as evidenced by written documents and records.

6. This Agreement shall be effective until _____ years after the date of this Agreement.

7. This Agreement shall be binding upon and shall inure to the benefit of the parties and their respective heirs, successors, assigns and legal representatives.

8. This Agreement shall be governed by the laws of the State of _____.

Discloser and Recipient, intending to be legally bound, have signed this Agreement on the date first indicated above.

_____   _____
Discloser's signature   Recipient's signature

19 Use and Registration of Trademarks

Function of Trademarks

The main function of a trademark is to indicate the origin or source of goods or services. A trademark is any word, name, symbol, device, or any combination thereof adopted and used by a manufacturer or merchant to identify his goods and to distinguish them from those manufactured or sold by others. A trademark may also function to symbolize or guarantee the quality of goods which bear the trademark. Rights in a trademark are acquired only by use of the trademark on particular goods. This right to use a trademark is a property interest that the trademark owner can assert to prevent others from using the mark or one which is confusingly similar.

Trademark rights are governed by both federal and state laws. This text will review only those rights granted by federal law and the means of acquiring such federal rights. Federal trademark law is governed by the Trademark Act of 1946, as amended, and the Trademark Rules of Practice. The Trademark Act of 1946 can be found in Title 15, Chapter 22 of the U.S. Code. The Trademark Rules of Practice can be found in Title 37 of the Code of Federal Regulations.

Federal registration of a trademark is not mandatory, but this registration does provide some major benefits to the trademark owner. To be eligible for federal registration, a trademark must actually be used in commerce, or the owner must have a bona fide intent to use the trademark in commerce. The intent to use a trademark can be extended for periods of six months up to a maximum of two years and is a good way for reserving a trademark with the U.S. Patent and Trademark Office. A trademark is deemed to be used in commerce when it is placed in any manner on goods or their containers or on tags or labels affixed thereto and the goods are sold or transported in interstate commerce.

Federal registration of a trademark recognizes the right of the trademark owner to use the trademark nationwide. The federal registration also serves as notice to all others of the trademark owner's rights in the trademark. Federal registration gives the trademark owner the right to use the registration symbol ®, which may deter others from using the trademark. Although the trademark owner is not required to use the ® symbol for registered trademarks, use of the ® symbol may be helpful in keeping the trademark from becoming generic. If the trademark has not been registered, you should use the symbol TM to protect your trademark rights under state law. Federal law also gives the trademark owner the right to sue unauthorized users of the trademark for an injunction, damages, or recovery of profits.

Registration of Trademarks

Federal law provides for the registration of trademarks on two types of registers, designated as the Principal Register and the Supplemental Register. Trademarks that are created, arbitrary, or fanciful may (if otherwise qualified) be registered on the Principal Register. A trademark that does not qualify for registration on the Principal Register may be registered on the Supplemental Register if it is capable of distinguishing applicant's goods and normally has been used in commerce for at least one year.

If all other requirements are satisfied, a trademark may be registered on the Principal Register unless it consists of a mark which: (1) when applied to the goods or services of the applicant is merely descriptive or deceptively misdescriptive of them; or (2) when applied to the goods or services of the applicant is primarily geographically descriptive or deceptively misdescriptive; or (3) is primarily a surname. Thus, the trademark "car" cannot be registered for an automobile, as this is merely descriptive of the goods. The trademark "America All-Wool" cannot be registered for a cotton garment made in Japan because it is deceptively misdescriptive. The trademark "Jones" normally cannot be registered as it is primarily a surname. As an exception to the general rules, the above marks may be registered on the Principal Register if they have become distinctive as applied to the applicant's goods in commerce. This usually requires proof of exclusive and continuous use of the mark by the applicant in commerce for the prior five years.

Trademarks capable of distinguishing applicant's goods or services and not registrable on the Principal Register, but which have been in lawful use in commerce by the applicant for one year immediately prior to filing for registration, may normally be registered on the Supplemental Register. For the purpose of registration on the Supplemental Register, a trademark may consist of any mark, symbol, name, word, slogan, phrase, label, package, configuration of goods, surname, geographical name, numeral, device, or any combination thereof, but such mark must be capable of distinguishing the applicant's good or services.

A trademark cannot be registered on either the Principal Register or the Supplemental Register if it:

(a) Consists of or comprises immoral, deceptive, or scandalous matter or matter which may disparage or falsely suggest a connection with persons, living or dead, institutions, beliefs, or national symbols, or bring them into contempt or disrepute.

(b) Consists of or comprises the flag or coat of arms or other insignia of the United States, or of any State or municipality, or of any foreign nation, or any simulation thereof.

(c) Consists of or comprises a name, portrait, or signature identifying a particular living individual, except by his or her written consent; or the name, signature, or portrait of a deceased President of the United States during the life of his widow or her widower, if any, except by the written consent of the widow or widower.

(d) Consists of or comprises a mark which so resembles a mark registered in the Patent and Trademark Office, or a mark or trade name previously used in the United States by another and not abandoned, as to be likely when applied to the goods of another person to cause confusion or to cause mistake or to deceive.

Federal law also provides for registration of service marks and certification marks. A service mark is a mark used in the sale or advertisement of services to identify the origin of the services. A certification mark is one used in connection with the products or services of persons other than the owner of the mark to certify the origin, quality, accuracy, or other characteristics of such goods or services.

Filing a Trademark Application
The owner of a trademark used or intended to be used in commerce may register the trademark by filing an application for

registrationin the U.S. Patent and Trademark Office. The application must be filed in the name of the trademark owner and comprises the following four parts:

1. a written application (A sample Trademark/Service Mark Application form is provided at the end of this chapter);

2. a drawing of the mark;

3. three specimens or facsimiles of the mark; and

4. the filing fee ($175.00 for registration in each class at the time of this printing).

The application must be in the English language and must specify:

(a) the name of the applicant;

(b) the citizenship of the applicant; if the applicant is a partnership, the names and citizenship of the general partners or, if the applicant is a corporation or association, the state or country under which it is organized;

(c) the domicile and post office address of the applicant;

(d) that the applicant has adopted and is actually using the mark shown in the drawing which accompanies the application, or that the applicant has a bona fide intention to use mark, in interstate commerce;

(e) the particular goods on or in connection with which the mark is used or is intended to be used;

(f) the class, according to the official classification, in which the goods or services fall, if known to the applicant (An International Classification list is provided later in this chapter);

(g) the date of applicant's first use of the mark, and the date of the applicant's first use of the mark in interstate commerce, if any; and

(h) the mode or manner in which the mark is or will be used.

The application must be signed and verified (sworn to) or include a declaration by the applicant or by a member of the firm or an officer of the corporation or association that is applying for registration of the trademark. The application for registration of a trademark may be made by the owner or by an attorney or other person authorized to practice before the Trademark Office.

The drawing must be a substantially exact representation of the mark as actually used or to be used in connection with the goods or services. The drawing of a mark may be dispensed with if the mark is not capable of representation by a drawing, but in such case the written application must contain an adequate description of the mark.

If the application is for registration of only a word, letter, or numeral, or any combination thereof, not depicted in special form, the drawing may be the mark typed in capital letters on paper.

The drawing must be made upon pure white durable paper that has a smooth surface. The size of the sheet on which a drawing is made must be 8 to 8 1/2 inches wide and 11 inches long. The size of the mark must be such as to leave a margin of at least 1 inch on the sides and bottom of the paper and at least 1 inch between it and the heading. The drawing can not be more than 4 inches high and 4 inches wide. Across the top of the drawing, beginning one inch from the top edge and not exceeding one third of the sheet, there must be a heading and, listed on separate lines, applicant's complete name, applicant's address, the dates of first use of the mark and first use of the mark in interstate commerce (if applicable), and the goods or services for which the mark is used. Dates of use of the mark are not required if the trademark registration is based on applicant's intent to use the mark.

A trademark may be placed in any manner on the goods, their containers or displays, or on tags or labels attached to the goods. The three specimens shall be duplicates of the actually used labels, tags, containers, or displays and shall be capable of being arranged flat and be of a size not larger than 8 1/2 by 11 inches. When, due to the manner of affixing or using the mark, specimens as stated above cannot be furnished, three copies of a suitable photograph or other acceptable reproduction within the above size requirements can be furnished.

It is recommended that a trademark search be carried out before a mark is used or an application for registration is filed. The Trademark Register of the United States, published yearly by Patent Searching Service, National Press Building, Suite 1297, Washington, D.C. 20045, provides a list of active registered U.S. trademarks.

If you are the owner of a trademark, you can file the trademark application yourself with the U.S. Patent and Trademark Office, Washington, D.C. 20231. The mark can be registered in one or more classes, but a separate application should be filed for each class. The filing fee at the time of this printing is $175 for each class. Typical attorney's fees for filing a trademark registration range from about $300 to $1000.

After your application has been examined, the U.S. Patent and Trademark Office will allow your registration if all requirements have been met and your mark is not confusingly similar to other marks. If your application has indicated a bona fide intent to use the mark, you must normally file a statement of actual use (along with dates of actual use, three specimens and the required fee) within six months after receiving a notice of allowance from the Patent and Trademark Office. After allowance, the mark is published for opposition and, if no opposition is filed, the mark is registered.

International Classification of Goods and Services

The following is a list of the classes of goods and services which you should designate in the application for registration of a trademark:

Goods

Class 1. Chemical products used in industry, science, photography, agriculture, horticulture, forestry; artificial and synthetic resins; plastics in the form of powders, liquids, or pastes, for industrial use; manures (natural and artificial); fire extinguishing compositions; tempering substances and chemical preparations for soldering; chemical substances for preserving foodstuffs, tanning substances; adhesive substances used in industry.

Class 2. Paints, varnishes, lacquers; preservatives against rust and against deterioration of wood; coloring matters, dyestuffs; mordants; natural resins; metals in foil and powder form for painters and decorators.

Class 3. Bleaching preparations and other substances for laundry use; cleaning, polishing, scouring, and abrasive preparations; soaps; perfumery, essential oils, cosmetics, hair lotions; dentifrices.

Class 4. Industrial oils and greases (other than oils and fats and essential oils); lubricants; dust laying and absorbing compositions; fuels (including motor spirits) and illuminants; candles, tapers, night lights, and wicks.

Class 5. Pharmaceutical, veterinary, and sanitary substances; infants' and invalids' foods; plasters, material for bandaging; material for stopping teeth, dental wax, disinfectants; preparations for killing weeds and destroying vermin, fungicides, and herbicides.

Class 6. Unwrought and partly wrought common metals and their alloys; anchors, anvils, balls, rolled and cast building materials; rails and other metallic materials for railway tracks; chains (except driving chains for vehicles); cables and wires (nonelectric); locksmiths' work; metallic pipes and tubes; safes and cash boxes; steel balls; horseshoes; nails and screws; other goods in nonprecious metal not included in other classes; ores.

Class 7. Machines and machine tools; motors (except for land vehicles); machine couplings and belting (except for land vehicles); large size agricultural implements; incubators.

Class 8. Hand tools and instruments; cutlery, forks, and spoons; side arms; razors.

Class 9. Scientific, nautical, surveying and electrical apparatus and instruments (including wireless), photographic, cinematographic, optical, weighing, measuring, signalling, checking (supervision), lifesaving, and teaching apparatus and instruments; apparatus for recording; automatic vending machines; coin or counterfreed apparatus; talking machines; cash registers; calculating machines; data-processing equipment; fire-extinguishing apparatus.

Class 10. Surgical, medical, dental, and veterinary instruments and apparatus (including artificial limbs, eyes, and teeth); suture materials.

Class 11. Apparatus for lighting, heating, steam generating, cooking, refrigerating, drying, ventilating, water supply, and sanitary purposes.

Class 12. Vehicles; apparatus for locomotion by land, air, or water.

Class 13. Firearms; ammunition and projectiles; explosive substances; fireworks.

Class 14. Precious metals and their alloys and goods made of precious metal or coated therewith (except cutlery, forks, and spoons); jewelry, precious stones, horological and other chronometric instruments.

Class 15. Musical instruments (other than talking machines and wireless apparatus).

Class 16. Paper, cardboard, articles of paper or of cardboard (not included in other classes); printed matter, newspapers and periodicals, books; book-binding material; photographs; stationery; adhesive materials (stationery); artists' materials; paint brushes; typewriters and office requisites (other than furniture); instructional and teaching material (other than apparatus); playing cards; printers' type and cliches (stereotype).

Class 17. Gutta-percha, rubber, balata and substitutes, articles made from these substances and not included in other classes; plastics in the form of sheets, blocks, and rods, being for use in manufacture; materials for packing, stopping, or insulating; asbestos, mica and their products; hose pipes (nonmetallic).

Class 18. Leather and imitations of leather, and articles made from these materials and not included in other classes; skins, hides; trunks and travelling bags; umbrellas, parasols, and walking sticks; whips, harness, and saddlery.

Class 19. Building materials, natural and artificial stone, cement, lime, mortar, plaster, and gravel; pipes of earthenware or cement; road-making materials; asphalt, pitch, and bitumen; nonmetallic portable buildings; stone monuments; chimney pots.

Class 20. Furniture, mirrors, picture frames; articles (not included in other classes) of wood, cork, reeds, cane, wicker, horn, bone, ivory, whalebone, shell, amber, mother-of-pearl, meerschaum, celluloid, plastic or substitutes for all these materials.

Class 21. Small domestic utensils and containers (neither made of precious metals nor coated therewith); combs and sponges; brushes (other than paint brushes); brush-making materials; instruments and material for cleaning purposes; steel wool; unworked or semi-worked glass (excluding glass used in building); glassware, porcelain, and earthenware, not included in other classes.

Class 22. Ropes, string, nets, tents, awnings, tarpaulins, sails, sacks; padding and stuffing materials (hair, kapok, feathers, seaweed, etc.); raw fibrous textile materials.

Class 23. Yarns, threads.

Class 24. Tissues (piece goods); bed and table covers; textile articles not included in other classes.

Class 25. Clothing, including boots, shoes and slippers, headgear.

Class 26. Lace and embroidery, ribbons and braid; buttons, press buttons, hooks and eyes, pins and needles; artificial flowers.

Class 27. Carpets, rugs, mats and matting; linoleums and other materials for covering existing floors; wall hangings (nontextile).

Class 28. Games and playthings; gymnastic and sporting articles (except clothing); ornaments and decorations for Christmas trees.

Class 29. Meats, fish, poultry, and game; meat extracts; preserves; dried and cooked fruits and vegetables; jellies, jams; eggs, milk and other dairy products; edible oils and fats; salad dressings; preserves, pickles.

Class 30. Coffee, tea, cocoa, sugar, rice, tapioca, sago, coffee substitutes; flour, preparations made from cereals; bread, biscuits, cakes, pastry and confectionery, ices; honey, treacle; yeast, baking powder; salt, mustard, pepper, vinegar, sauces (excluding salad dressings), spices; ice.

Class 31. Agricultural, horticultural, and forestry products and grains not included in other classes; living animals; fresh fruits and vegetables; seeds; live plants and flowers; foodstuffs for animals; malt.

Class 32. Beer, ale and porter; mineral and aerated waters and other nonalcoholic drinks; syrups and other preparations for making beverages; fruit drinks and fruit juices.

Class 33. Wines, spirits, and liqueurs, alcoholic beverages (excluding beers). Class 34. Tobacco, raw or manufactured; smokers' articles; matches.

Services
Class 35. Advertising and business.
Class 36. Insurance and financial.
Class 37. Construction and repair.
Class 38. Communication.
Class 39. Transportation and storage.

Class 40. Material treatment.
Class 41. Education and entertainment.
Class 42. Miscellaneous (includes services which do not fit in other classes).

Checklist for Registering a Trademark

❏ Identify trademark that you would like to use and conduct a trademark search to see if anyone else is using the mark.

❏ Complete and sign trademark application.

❏ If mark is currently used in interstate commerce, include three specimens of the mark as actually used and indicate the dates of first use in the trademark application.

❏ If mark is not currently used in interstate commerce, indicate that you have a bona fide intention to use the mark in such commerce. (After receiving notice of allowance a statement of actual use must be filed along with three specimens and required fee within six months. However, this period can be extended up to two years by filing a request for extension and paying the required fee to the U.S. Patent and Trademark Office.)

❏ File the completed trademark application, three specimens, and the application fee with U.S. Department of Commerce, Patent and Trademark Office, Washington, D.C. 20231. (The application fee at the time of this printing is $175 for each class.)

❏ Respond to communications from the U.S. Patent and Trademark Office within the time provided.

❏ Consult an attorney if your trademark registration involves complex or difficult issues.

Trademark/Service Mark Application, Principal Register, with Declaration

Mark (Identify the mark) _____   Class No. (If known) _____

To the Assistant Secretary and Commissioner of Patents and Trademarks:

Applicant Name: _____

Applicant Entity: (Check one and supply requested information)

❏   Individual — Citizenship (Country): _____

❏   Partnership — Partnership Domicile (State and Country): _____

Names and Citizenship (Country) of General Partners: _____

_____

❏   Corporation — State (Country, if appropriate) of Incorporation: _____

❏   Other (Specify Nature of Entity and Domicile): _____

_____

Goods and/or Services:

Applicant requests registration of the above-identified trademark/service mark shown in the accompanying drawing in the United States Patent and Trademark Office on the Principal Register established by the Act of July 5, 1946 (15 U.S.C. 1051 et. seq., as amended.) for the following goods/services:_____

_____

_____

Basis for Application: (Check one or more, but not both the first and second boxes, and supply requested information)

❏   Applicant is using the mark in commerce on or in connection with the above identified goods/services. (15 U.S.C. 105(a), as amended.) Three specimens showing the mark as used in commerce are submitted with this application.

•   Date of first use of the mark anywhere _____

•   Date of first use of the mark in commerce which the U.S. Congress may regulate:_____

•   Specify the type of commerce _____
        (e.g., interstate, between the U.S. and a specified foreign country)

•   Specify manner or mode of use of mark on or in connection with the goods/services _____

_____
(e.g., trademark is applied to labels, service mark is used in advertisements)

❏   Applicant has a bona fide intention to use the mark in commerce on or in connection with the above identified goods/ services. (15 U.S.C. 1051(b), as amended.)

•   Specify intended manner or mode of use of mark on or in connection with the goods or services:

_____
(e.g., trademark will be applied to labels, service mark will be used in advertisements)

❏ Applicant has a bona fide intention to use the mark in commerce on or in connection with the above identified goods/services, and asserts a claim of priority based upon a foreign application in accordance with 15 U.S.C. 1126(d), as amended.

Country of foreign filing: _____ Date of foreign filing:_____

❏ Applicant has a bona fide intention to use the mark in commerce on or in connection with the above identified goods/services and, accompanying this application, submits a certification or certified copy of a foreign registration in accordance with 15 U.S.C. 1126(e), as amended.

Country of registration:_____ Registration number: _____

Declaration

The undersigned being hereby warned that willful false statements and the like so made are punishable by fine or imprisonment, or both, under 18 U.S.C. 1001, and that such willful false statements may jeopardize the validity of the application or any resulting registration, declares that he/she is properly authorized to execute this application on behalf of the applicant; he/she believes the applicant to be the owner of the trademark/service mark sought to be registered, or, if the application is being filed under 15 U.S.C. 105(b), he/she believes applicant to be entitled to use such mark in commerce; to the best of his/her knowledge and belief no other person, firm, corporation, or association has the right to use the above identified mark in commerce, either in the identical form thereof or in such near resemblance thereto as to be likely, when used on or in connection with the goods/services of such other person, to cause confusion, or to cause mistake, or to deceive; and that all statements made of his/her own knowledge are true and all statements made on information and belief are believed to be true.

_____   _____
Signature   Date

_____   _____
Print or Type Name and Position   Telephone

Other Information for Applicant

To receive a filing date, the application must be completed and signed by the applicant and submitted along with:

1. The prescribed fee for each class of goods/services listed in the application;
2. A drawing of the mark in conformance with 37 CFR 2.52;
3. If the application is based on use of the mark in commerce, three (3) specimens (evidence) of the mark as used in commerce for each class of goods/services listed in the application. All three specimens may be the same and may be in the nature of: (a) labels showing the mark which are placed on the goods; (b) a photograph of the mark as it appears on the goods; (c) brochures or advertisements showing the mark as used in connection with the services.

Verification of the application - The application must be signed in order for the application to receive a filing date. Only the following person may sign the verification (Declaration) for the application, depending on the applicant's legal entity: (a) the individual applicant; (b) an officer of the corporate applicant; (c) one general partner of a partnership applicant; (d) all joint applicants.

Additional information concerning the requirements for filing an application are available in a booklet entitled Basic Facts about Trademarks, which may be obtained by writing:

U.S. Department of Commerce Patent and Trademark Office Washington, D.C. 20231
Or by calling: (703) 557-INFO

20 *Copyrights to Your Writings and Artistic Works*

Introducing You to Copyrights

Copyright is a right granted by federal law to the author or creator of literary or artistic works. It gives you as the author the sole privilege of reproducing and selling your work as well as the right to prevent others from copying or selling the work without your permission. This right covers works such as writings, paintings, photographs, sound recordings, motion pictures, music, and computer programs.

The Federal Copyright Act preempts copyright protection under state law for those works that are subject to federal copyright protection. This means that federal copyright protection is the only copyright protection available for these works.

The materials that follow will discuss the general law of copyright and the procedure for copyright registration for:

- a work of the performing arts,

- a nondramatic literary work,

- a work of the visual arts, and

- a sound recording.

The fee for applying for copyright registration at the time of this printing is $20 Typical legal fees for copyright registration range from about $100 to $500.

Scope of Copyright Protection

A copyright gives you the sole right to control the reproduction and distribution of your copyrighted work. You have the right to prevent others from reproducing the work without your permission.

Copyright does not prevent others from using the ideas or information revealed by your work. Copyright protects only the literary, musical, artistic, or graphic form in which you express your work. Anyone is free to use your concepts, and may create his or her own expression of the same concepts as long as he or she does not copy your form of expression.

Under the Copyright Act, the owner of a copyright has the exclusive rights to do and to authorize any of the following:

- to reproduce the copyrighted work in copies or phonorecords;

- to prepare derivative works based upon the copyrighted work (examples of derivative works are translations, musical arrangements, dramatizations, motion picture versions, sound recording, abridgments, condensations, or any other forms in which a work may be recast, transformed, or adapted);

- to distribute copies or phonorecords of the copyrighted work to the public by

145

sale or other transfer of ownership, or by rental, lease, or lending;

- to perform the copyrighted work publicly;

- to display the copyrighted work publicly.

Anyone who violates any of the exclusive rights of the copyright owner is an infringer of the copyright. The copyright owner may recover from the infringer statutory damages (which are an amount awarded in the discretion of the court) or actual damages plus any profits of the infringer. The copyright owner may also recover court costs and attorney fees from the infringer if allowed by the court. The copyright owner may also obtain an injunction to prevent and restrain infringement of his or her copyright. Registration of the copyrighted work prior to the infringement is necessary to be eligible for statutory damages, court costs, and attorneys' fees. Copyright registration must also be obtained before any copyright infringement action can be brought. Copyright infringement actions must be brought within three years after the infringement takes place or should have been discovered.

Fair use of copyrighted works does not amount to copyright infringement. Fair use for purposes such as criticism, comment, news reporting, teaching (including multiple copies for classroom use), scholarship, or research is not an infringement of copyright.

Libraries may reproduce one copy of the copyrighted work if it is made without commercial advantage, the library is open to the public, and the reproduction includes a notice of copyright. This use by the libraries is not an infringement of copyright.

Copyright does not protect any idea, procedure, process, system, method of operation, concept, principle, or discovery. Copyright protects only the form of expression.

For works created after January 1, 1978, the duration of the copyright will be the life of the author plus 50 years after the author's death.

Subject Matter of Copyright Protection

The Copyright Act permits copyright protection for original works of authorship. Seven types of works are listed that may be protected by copyright. These works include the following:

- literary works;

- musical works, including any accompanying words;

- dramatic works, including any accompanying music;

- pantomimes and choreographic works;

- pictoral, graphic, and sculptural works;

- motion pictures and other audiovisual works;

- sound recordings.

Other works not listed above may also be protected by copyright if they meet the definition of "original works of authorship."

Literary works are works, other than audiovisual works, that are expressed in words, numbers, or other verbal or numerical symbols, such as books, magazines, manuscripts, directories, catalogs, cards, and computer programs.

Musical works would include written musical arrangements, lyrics, and songs.

Dramatic works would include written plays and any written music that is a part thereof.

Pantomimes and choreographic works include physical expressions and dance.

Pictoral, graphic, and sculptural works include two and three-dimensional works of art, photographs, paintings, sketches, prints, maps, globes, charts, designs, technical drawings, diagrams, and models.

Motion picture and audiovisual works include films, movies, and video recordings.

Sound recordings are works that result

from fixation of a series of musical, spoken, or other sounds, such as discs, tapes, and phonorecords, but do not include the sounds accompanying a motion picture or other audiovisual work.

Copyright protection is only available for original works of authorship. The originality requirement means that the work must be the independent creation of the person seeking copyright protection. The test for originality is met if the work owes its origin to the author and is independently created and not copied from other works. The mere fact that someone else has created something similar will not prevent you from obtaining copyright protection on your independent creation.

Copyright protection does not extend to names, titles, and slogans. These can be appropriately protected by trademark.

To qualify for federal copyright protection, the works of authorship must be fixed in a tangible form. This means that the work must be in a physical form such that it can be reproduced or otherwise communicated. Thus a mere idea or other abstract and imaginary creations cannot be copyrighted.

A work is given copyright when it is fixed in a copy or phonorecord for the first time. Publication is the distribution of copies or phonorecords of a work to the public by sale, rental, lease, or lending.

Copyright Notice

The copyright law requires a specific notice to enable the owner to obtain the strongest copyright protection for published works. If you plan to publish or publicly distribute your work, you can place a copyright notice on all such copies. Use of the copyright notice does not require the permission of the Copyright Office. The copyright notice may be used even if the work has not been registered with the U.S. Copyright Office. However, keep in mind that definitely since March 1989 and in some cases from 1978 to 1989 you will not lose your copyright if you fail to put copyright notice on your work. The benefit of a copyright notice is that infringers cannot ask the court to lessen damages because they were unaware of your copyright.

The copyright notice consists of three parts: (1) the symbol "©" or the word "copyright" or the abbreviation "copr."; (2) the year of first publication; and (3) the name of the copyright owner. For example, the proper notice could follow these forms:

Copyright 1991 Carl W. Battle
© Carl W. Battle 1991
Copr. 1991 C. W. Battle

The notice should be affixed to the copies in such a manner and location as to give reasonable notice of the claim of copyright.

For phonograph records the notice can consist of (1) the symbol ℗; (2) the year of first publication; and (3) the name of the copyright owner.

Registering Your Copyright

Use of Form PA for Work of the Performing Arts: Form PA is used for copyright registration covering works of the performing arts. A sample Form PA is provided at the end of this chapter along with line by line instructions. The instructions are also useful for Forms SR, TX, and VA where applicable. This category includes works prepared for the purpose of being performed directly or indirectly before an audience.

Examples of works of the performing arts are:

- musical works, including any accompanying words;

- dramatic works, including any accompanying music;

- pantomimes and choreographic works;

- motion pictures and other audiovisual works.

Along with the application for copyright

registration, submit two complete copies of the published work. Submit one complete copy if the work is unpublished. Be sure to sign the application form.

Use of Form SR for Sound Recording: Form SR is used for copyright registration covering a sound recording. A sample Form SR is provided at the end of this chapter. This form should be used when the copyright claim is limited to the sound recording itself. Sound recordings are works that result from the creation of a series of musical, spoken, or other sounds. Sound recordings do not include the sounds that accompany a motion picture or other audiovisual work.

Along with the application for copyright registration, submit two complete phonorecords or recordings of the published work along with any printed material. Submit one phonorecord or recording if the work is unpublished. Be sure to sign the application form.

Use of Form TX for Nondramatic Literary Work: Form TX is used for copyright registration covering nondramatic literary works. A sample Form TX is provided at the end of this chapter. This category includes all types of works written in words or other symbols, except dramatic works and audiovisual works. Examples of nondramatic literary works are books, poetry, magazines, directories, catalogs, advertising copy, and compilations of information.

Along with the application for copyright registration, submit two complete copies of the published work. Submit one complete copy if the work is unpublished. Be sure to sign the application form.

Use of Form VA for Work of the Visual Arts: Form VA is used for copyright registration covering works of the visual arts. A sample Form VA is provided at the end of this chapter. This category includes pictoral, graphic, and sculptural works such as paintings, photographs, prints, art reproductions, maps, charts, diagrams, technical drawings,

labels, and advertisements.

Along with the application for copyright registration, submit two complete copies of the published work. Submit one copy if the work is unpublished. If the work is unique or a limited edition, you can submit photos, photocopies or other identifying materials instead of an original copy. Be sure to sign the application form.

Checklist for Registering a Copyright

❏ Fill out appropriate application form. (Use a typewriter or print in dark ink.)

❏ Use one of the following forms:

- Form PA — Works of the Performing Arts
- Form SR — Sound Recordings
- Form TX — Nondramatic Literary Work
- Form VA — Work of the Visual Arts

❏ Sign the form in the space provided for certification.

❏ Enclose with the application a check or money order for the $20 application fee payable to: Register of Copyrights.

❏ Mail completed application and the necessary copies of the work to:

Register of Copyrights
Library of Congress
Washington, DC 20559

❏ Consult an attorney if your copyright involves difficult or complex issues.

Ⓔ Filling Out Application Form TX

Detach and read these instructions before completing this form. Make sure all applicable spaces have been filled in before you return this form.

BASIC INFORMATION

When to Use This Form: Use Form TX for registration of published or unpublished non-dramatic literary works, excluding periodicals or serial issues. This class includes a wide variety of works: fiction, non-fiction, poetry, textbooks, reference works, directories, catalogs, advertising copy, compilations of information, and computer programs. For periodicals and serials, use Form SE.

Deposit to Accompany Application: An application for copyright registration must be accompanied by a deposit consisting of copies or phonorecords representing the entire work for which registration is to be made. The following are the general deposit requirements as set forth in the statute:

Unpublished Work: Deposit one complete copy (or phonorecord).

Published Work: Deposit two complete copies (or phonorecords) of the best edition.

Work First Published Outside the United States: Deposit one complete copy (or phonorecord) of the first foreign edition.

Contribution to a Collective Work: Deposit one complete copy (or phonorecord) of the best edition of the collective work.

The Copyright Notice: For works first published on or after March 1, 1989, the law provides that a copyright notice on a specified form "may be placed on all publicly distributed copies from which the work can be visually perceived." Use of the copyright notice is the responsibility of the copyright owner and does not require advance permission from the Copyright Office. The required form of the notice for copies generally consists of three elements: (1) the symbol "©", or the word "Copyright," or the abbreviation "Copr."; (2) the year of first publication; and (3) the name of the owner of copyright. For example: "© 1989 Jane Cole." The notice is to be affixed to the copies "in such manner and location as to give reasonable notice of the claim of copyright." Works first published prior to March 1, 1989, **must** carry the notice or risk loss of copyright protection.

For information about notice requirements for works published before March 1, 1989, or other copyright information, write: Information Section, LM-401, Copyright Office, Library of Congress, Washington, D.C. 20559.

LINE-BY-LINE INSTRUCTIONS

1 SPACE 1: Title

Title of This Work: Every work submitted for copyright registration must be given a title to identify that particular work. If the copies or phonorecords of the work bear a title (or an identifying phrase that could serve as a title), transcribe that wording *completely* and *exactly* on the application. Indexing of the registration and future identification of the work will depend on the information you give here.

Previous or Alternative Titles: Complete this space if there are any additional titles for the work under which someone searching for the registration might be likely to look, or under which a document pertaining to the work might be recorded.

Publication as a Contribution: If the work being registered is a contribution to a periodical, serial, or collection, give the title of the contribution in the "Title of this Work" space. Then, in the line headed "Publication as a Contribution," give information about the collective work in which the contribution appeared.

2 SPACE 2: Author(s)

General Instructions: After reading these instructions, decide who are the "authors" of this work for copyright purposes. Then, unless the work is a "collective work," give the requested information about every "author" who contributed any appreciable amount of copyrightable matter to this version of the work. If you need further space, request additional Continuation sheets. In the case of a collective work, such as an anthology, collection of essays, or encyclopedia, give information about the author of the collective work as a whole.

Name of Author: The fullest form of the author's name should be given. Unless the work was "made for hire," the individual who actually created the work is its "author." In the case of a work made for hire, the statute provides that "the employer or other person for whom the work was prepared is considered the author."

What is a "Work Made for Hire"? A "work made for hire" is defined as: (1) "a work prepared by an employee within the scope of his or her employment"; or (2) "a work specially ordered or commissioned for use as a contribution to a collective work, as a part of a motion picture or other audiovisual work, as a translation, as a supplementary work, as a compilation, as an instructional text, as a test, as answer material for a test, or as an atlas, if the parties expressly agree in a written instrument signed by them that the work shall be considered a work made for hire." If you have checked "Yes" to indicate that the work was "made for hire," you must give the full legal name of the employer (or other person for whom the work was prepared). You may also include the name of the employee along with the name of the employer (for example: "Elster Publishing Co., employer for hire of John Ferguson").

"Anonymous" or "Pseudonymous" Work: An author's contribution to a work is "anonymous" if that author is not identified on the copies or phonorecords of the work. An author's contribution to a work is "pseudonymous" if that author is identified on the copies or phonorecords under a fictitious name. If the work is "anonymous" you may: (1) leave the line blank; or (2) state " anonymous" on the line; or (3) reveal the author's identity. If the work is "pseudonymous" you may : (1) leave the line blank; or (2) give the pseudonym and identify it as such (for example: "Huntley Haverstock, pseudonym"); or (3) reveal the author's name, making clear which is the real name and which is the pseudonym (for example: "Judith Barton, whose pseudonym is Madeline Elster"). However, the citizenship or domicile of the author **must** be given in all cases.

Dates of Birth and Death: If the author is dead, the statute requires that the year of death be included in the application unless the work is anonymous or pseudonymous. The author's birth date is optional, but is useful as a form of identification. Leave this space blank if the author's contribution was a "work made for hire."

Author's Nationality or Domicile: Give the country of which the author is a citizen, or the country in which the author is domiciled. Nationality or domicile **must** be given in all cases.

Nature of Authorship: After the words "Nature of Authorship" give a brief general statement of the nature of this particular author's contribution to the work. Examples: "Entire text"; "Coauthor of entire text"; "Chapters 11-14"; "Editorial revisions"; "Compilation and English translation"; "New text."

3 SPACE 3: Creation and Publication

General Instructions: Do not confuse "creation" with "publication." Every application for copyright registration must state "the year in which creation of the work was completed." Give the date and nation of first publication only if the work has been published.

Creation: Under the statute, a work is "created" when it is fixed in a copy or phonorecord for the first time. Where a work has been prepared over a period of time, the part of the work existing in fixed form on a particular date constitutes the created work on that date. The date you give here should be the year in which the author completed the particular version for which registration is now being sought, even if other versions exist or if further changes or additions are planned.

Publication: The statute defines "publication" as "the distribution of copies or phonorecords of a work to the public by sale or other transfer of ownership, or by rental, lease, or lending"; a work is also "published" if there has been an "offering to distribute copies or phonorecords to a group of persons for purposes of further distribution, public performance, or public display." Give the full date (month, day, year) when, and the country where, publication first occurred. If first publication took place simultaneously in the United States and other countries, it is sufficient to state "U.S.A."

4 SPACE 4: Claimant(s)

Name(s) and Address(es) of Copyright Claimant(s): Give the name(s) and address(es) of the copyright claimant(s) in this work even if the claimant is the same as the author. Copyright in a work belongs initially to the author of the work (including, in the case of a work made for hire, the employer or other person for whom the work was prepared). The copyright claimant is either the author of the work or a person or organization to whom the copyright initially belonging to the author has been transferred.

Transfer: The statute provides that, if the copyright claimant is not the author, the application for registration must contain "a brief statement of how the claimant obtained ownership of the copyright." If any copyright claimant named in space 4 is not an author named in space 2, give a brief, general statement summarizing the means by which that claimant obtained ownership of the copyright. Examples: "By written contract"; "Transfer of all rights by author"; "Assignment"; "By will." Do not attach transfer documents or other attachments or riders.

5 SPACE 5: Previous Registration

General Instructions: The questions in space 5 are intended to find out whether an earlier registration has been made for this work and, if so, whether there is any basis for a new registration. As a general rule, only one basic copyright registration can be made for the same version of a particular work.

Same Version: If this version is substantially the same as the work covered by a previous registration, a second registration is not generally possible unless: (1) the work has been registered in unpublished form and a second registration is now being sought to cover this first published edition; or (2) someone other than the author is identified as copyright claimant in the earlier registration, and the author is now seeking registration in his or her own name. If either of these two exceptions apply, check the appropriate box and give the earlier registration number and date. Otherwise, do not submit Form TX; instead, write the Copyright Office for information about supplementary registration or recordation of transfers of copyright ownership.

Changed Version: If the work has been changed, and you are now seeking registration to cover the additions or revisions, check the last box in space 5, give the earlier registration number and date, and complete both parts of space 6 in accordance with the instructions below.

Previous Registration Number and Date: If more than one previous registration has been made for the work, give the number and date of the latest registration.

6 SPACE 6: Derivative Work or Compilation

General Instructions: Complete space 6 if this work is a "changed version," "compilation," or "derivative work," and if it incorporates one or more earlier works that have already been published or registered for copyright, or that have fallen into the public domain. A "compilation" is defined as "a work formed by the collection and assembling of preexisting materials or of data that are selected, coordinated, or arranged in such a way that the resulting work as a whole constitutes an original work of authorship." A "derivative work" is "a work based on one or more preexisting works." Examples of derivative works include translations, fictionalizations, abridgments, condensations, or "any other form in which a work may be recast, transformed, or adapted." Derivative works also include works "consisting of editorial revisions, annotations, or other modifications" if these changes, as a whole, represent an original work of authorship.

Preexisting Material (space 6a): For derivative works, complete this space and space 6b. In space 6a identify the preexisting work that has been recast, transformed, or adapted. An example of preexisting material might be: "Russian version of Goncharov's 'Oblomov'." Do not complete space 6a for compilations.

Material Added to This Work (space 6b): Give a brief, general statement of the new material covered by the copyright claim for which registration is sought. **Derivative work** examples include: "Foreword, editing, critical annotations"; "Translation"; "Chapters 11-17." If the work is a **compilation**, describe both the compilation itself and the material that has been compiled. Example: "Compilation of certain 1917 Speeches by Woodrow Wilson." A work may be both a derivative work and compilation, in which case a sample statement might be: "Compilation and additional new material."

7 SPACE 7: Manufacturing Provisions

Due to the expiration of the Manufacturing Clause of the copyright law on June 30, 1986, this space has been deleted.

8 SPACE 8: Reproduction for Use of Blind or Physically Handicapped Individuals

General Instructions: One of the major programs of the Library of Congress is to provide Braille editions and special recordings of works for the exclusive use of the blind and physically handicapped. In an effort to simplify and speed up the copyright licensing procedures that are a necessary part of this program, section 710 of the copyright statute provides for the establishment of a voluntary licensing system to be tied in with copyright registration. Copyright Office regulations provide that you may grant a license for such reproduction and distribution solely for the use of persons who are certified by competent authority as unable to read normal printed material as a result of physical limitations. The license is entirely voluntary, nonexclusive, and may be terminated upon 90 days notice.

How to Grant the License: If you wish to grant it, check one of the three boxes in space 8. Your check in one of these boxes, together with your signature in space 10, will mean that the Library of Congress can proceed to reproduce and distribute under the license without further paperwork. For further information, write for Circular R63.

9,10,11 SPACE 9, 10, 11: Fee, Correspondence, Certification, Return Address

Deposit Account: If you maintain a Deposit Account in the Copyright Office, identify it in space 9. Otherwise leave the space blank and send the fee of $10 with your application and deposit.

Correspondence (space 9): This space should contain the name, address, area code, and telephone number of the person to be consulted if correspondence about this application becomes necessary.

Certification (space 10): The application can not be accepted unless it bears the date and the **handwritten signature** of the author or other copyright claimant, or of the owner of exclusive right(s), or of the duly authorized agent of author, claimant, or owner of exclusive right(s).

Address for Return of Certificate (space 11): The address box must be completed legibly since the certificate will be returned in a window envelope.

FORM TX

UNITED STATES COPYRIGHT OFFICE

REGISTRATION NUMBER

_____

TX _____ TXU _____

EFFECTIVE DATE OF REGISTRATION

_____

| Month | Day | Year |

DO NOT WRITE ABOVE THIS LINE. IF YOU NEED MORE SPACE, USE A SEPARATE CONTINUATION SHEET.

1 TITLE OF THIS WORK ▼

PREVIOUS OR ALTERNATIVE TITLES ▼

PUBLICATION AS A CONTRIBUTION If this work was published as a contribution to a periodical, serial, or collection, give information about the collective work in which the contribution appeared. **Title of Collective Work ▼**

If published in a periodical or serial give: **Volume ▼**   **Number ▼**   **Issue Date ▼**   **On Pages ▼**

2 NAME OF AUTHOR ▼

DATES OF BIRTH AND DEATH
Year Born ▼   Year Died ▼

Was this contribution to the work a "work made for hire"?
☐ Yes
☐ No

AUTHOR'S NATIONALITY OR DOMICILE
Name of Country
OR { Citizen of ▶_____
Domiciled in ▶_____

WAS THIS AUTHOR'S CONTRIBUTION TO THE WORK
Anonymous?   ☐ Yes ☐ No
Pseudonymous?   ☐ Yes ☐ No
If the answer to either of these questions is "Yes," see detailed instructions

NATURE OF AUTHORSHIP Briefly describe nature of the material created by this author in which copyright is claimed. ▼

NAME OF AUTHOR ▼

DATES OF BIRTH AND DEATH
Year Born ▼   Year Died ▼

Was this contribution to the work a "work made for hire"?
☐ Yes
☐ No

AUTHOR'S NATIONALITY OR DOMICILE
Name of Country
OR { Citizen of ▶_____
Domiciled in ▶_____

WAS THIS AUTHOR'S CONTRIBUTION TO THE WORK
Anonymous?   ☐ Yes ☐ No
Pseudonymous?   ☐ Yes ☐ No
If the answer to either of these questions is "Yes," see detailed instructions

NATURE OF AUTHORSHIP Briefly describe nature of the material created by this author in which copyright is claimed. ▼

NAME OF AUTHOR ▼

DATES OF BIRTH AND DEATH
Year Born ▼   Year Died ▼

Was this contribution to the work a "work made for hire"?
☐ Yes
☐ No

AUTHOR'S NATIONALITY OR DOMICILE
Name of Country
OR { Citizen of ▶_____
Domiciled in ▶_____

WAS THIS AUTHOR'S CONTRIBUTION TO THE WORK
Anonymous?   ☐ Yes ☐ No
Pseudonymous?   ☐ Yes ☐ No
If the answer to either of these questions is "Yes," see detailed instructions

NATURE OF AUTHORSHIP Briefly describe nature of the material created by this author in which copyright is claimed. ▼

3 YEAR IN WHICH CREATION OF THIS WORK WAS COMPLETED
◄ Year
This information must be given in all cases.

DATE AND NATION OF FIRST PUBLICATION OF THIS PARTICULAR WORK
Complete this information Month ▶_____ Day ▶_____ Year ▶_____
ONLY if this work has been published.   ◄ Nation

4 COPYRIGHT CLAIMANT(S) Name and address must be given even if the claimant is the same as the author given in space 2.▼

TRANSFER If the claimant(s) named here in space 4 are different from the author(s) named in space 2, give a brief statement of how the claimant(s) obtained ownership of the copyright.▼

See instructions before completing this space

DO NOT WRITE HERE OFFICE USE ONLY

APPLICATION RECEIVED

ONE DEPOSIT RECEIVED

TWO DEPOSITS RECEIVED

REMITTANCE NUMBER AND DATE

MORE ON BACK ▶ • Complete all applicable spaces (numbers 5-11) on the reverse side of this page.
• See detailed instructions.   • Sign the form at line 10.

DO NOT WRITE HERE

DO NOT WRITE ABOVE THIS LINE. IF YOU NEED MORE SPACE, USE A SEPARATE CONTINUATION SHEET.

PREVIOUS REGISTRATION   Has registration for this work, or for an earlier version of this work, already been made in the Copyright Office?

☐ Yes ☐ No   If your answer is "Yes," why is another registration being sought? (Check appropriate box) ▼

☐ This is the first published edition of a work previously registered in unpublished form.

☐ This is the first application submitted by this author as copyright claimant.

☐ This is a changed version of the work, as shown by space 6 on this application.

If your answer is "Yes," give: **Previous Registration Number** ▼   **Year of Registration** ▼

5

DERIVATIVE WORK OR COMPILATION   Complete both space 6a & 6b for a derivative work; complete only 6b for a compilation.
  a. Preexisting Material   Identify any preexisting work or works that this work is based on or incorporates. ▼

  b. Material Added to This Work   Give a brief, general statement of the material that has been added to this work and in which copyright is claimed. ▼

6

See instructions
before completing
this space

—space deleted—

7

REPRODUCTION FOR USE OF BLIND OR PHYSICALLY HANDICAPPED INDIVIDUALS   A signature on this form at space 10, and a
check in one of the boxes here in space 8, constitutes a non-exclusive grant of permission to the Library of Congress to reproduce and distribute solely for the blind
and physically handicapped and under the conditions and limitations prescribed by the regulations of the Copyright Office: (1) copies of the work identified in space
1 of this application in Braille (or similar tactile symbols); or (2) phonorecords embodying a fixation of a reading of that work; or (3) both.

  a ☐ Copies and Phonorecords   **b** ☐ Copies Only   **c** ☐ Phonorecords Only

8

See instructions

DEPOSIT ACCOUNT   If the registration fee is to be charged to a Deposit Account established in the Copyright Office, give name and number of Account.
Name ▼   **Account Number** ▼

9

CORRESPONDENCE   Give name and address to which correspondence about this application should be sent.   Name/Address/Apt/City/State/Zip ▼

Area Code & Telephone Number ▶

Be sure to
give your
daytime phone
◀ number

**CERTIFICATION*   I, the undersigned, hereby certify that I am the

Check one ▶

☐ author
☐ other copyright claimant
☐ owner of exclusive right(s)
☐ authorized agent of _____

of the work identified in this application and that the statements made
by me in this application are correct to the best of my knowledge.

Name of author or other copyright claimant, or owner of exclusive right(s) ▲

10

Typed or printed name and date ▼ If this is a published work, this date must be the same as or later than the date of publication given in space 3.

_____   **date ▶** _____

☞   Handwritten signature (X) ▼

* 17 U S C § 506(e) Any person who knowingly makes a false representation of a material fact in the application for copyright registration provided for by section 409, or in any written statement filed in
connection with the application shall be fined not more than $2 500

April 1989—200,000

☆ U.S. GOVERNMENT PRINTING OFFICE: 1989—241-428/80,018

FORM SR

UNITED STATES COPYRIGHT OFFICE

REGISTRATION NUMBER

_____

| SR | | SRU |

EFFECTIVE DATE OF REGISTRATION

_____

Month   Day   Year

DO NOT WRITE ABOVE THIS LINE. IF YOU NEED MORE SPACE, USE A SEPARATE CONTINUATION SHEET.

1

TITLE OF THIS WORK ▼

_____

PREVIOUS OR ALTERNATIVE TITLES ▼

_____

NATURE OF MATERIAL RECORDED ▼ See instructions

☐ Musical   ☐ Musical-Dramatic

☐ Dramatic   ☐ Literary

☐ Other _____

2

a

NAME OF AUTHOR ▼

DATES OF BIRTH AND DEATH
Year Born ▼   Year Died ▼

Was this contribution to the work a "work made for hire"?
☐ Yes
☐ No

AUTHOR'S NATIONALITY OR DOMICILE
Name of Country
OR { Citizen of ▶ _____
{ Domiciled in ▶ _____

WAS THIS AUTHOR'S CONTRIBUTION TO THE WORK
Anonymous? ☐ Yes ☐ No
Pseudonymous? ☐ Yes ☐ No
If the answer to either of these questions is "Yes," see detailed instructions

NATURE OF AUTHORSHIP Briefly describe nature of the material created by this author in which copyright is claimed. ▼

NOTE

Under the law, the "author" of a "work made for hire" is generally the employer, not the employee (see instructions). For any part of this work that was "made for hire" check "Yes" in the space provided, give the employer (or other person for whom the work was prepared) as "Author" of that part, and leave the space for dates of birth and death blank.

b

NAME OF AUTHOR ▼

DATES OF BIRTH AND DEATH
Year Born ▼   Year Died ▼

Was this contribution to the work a "work made for hire"?
☐ Yes
☐ No

AUTHOR'S NATIONALITY OR DOMICILE
Name of country
OR { Citizen of ▶ _____
{ Domiciled in ▶ _____

WAS THIS AUTHOR'S CONTRIBUTION TO THE WORK
Anonymous? ☐ Yes ☐ No
Pseudonymous? ☐ Yes ☐ No
If the answer to either of these questions is "Yes," see detailed instructions.

NATURE OF AUTHORSHIP Briefly describe nature of the material created by this author in which copyright is claimed. ▼

c

NAME OF AUTHOR ▼

DATES OF BIRTH AND DEATH
Year Born ▼   Year Died ▼

Was this contribution to the work a "work made for hire"?
☐ Yes
☐ No

AUTHOR'S NATIONALITY OR DOMICILE
Name of Country
OR { Citizen of ▶ _____
{ Domiciled in ▶ _____

WAS THIS AUTHOR'S CONTRIBUTION TO THE WORK
Anonymous? ☐ Yes ☐ No
Pseudonymous? ☐ Yes ☐ No
If the answer to either of these questions is "Yes," see detailed instructions

NATURE OF AUTHORSHIP Briefly describe nature of the material created by this author in which copyright is claimed. ▼

3

a **YEAR IN WHICH CREATION OF THIS WORK WAS COMPLETED** This information must be given in all cases.
◀ Year

b **DATE AND NATION OF FIRST PUBLICATION OF THIS PARTICULAR WORK**
Complete this information ONLY if this work has been published.
Month ▶ _____ Day ▶ _____ Year ▶ _____
◀ Nation

4

See instructions before completing this space.

COPYRIGHT CLAIMANT(S) Name and address must be given even if the claimant is the same as the author given in space 2.▼

TRANSFER If the claimant(s) named here in space 4 are different from the author(s) named in space 2, give a brief statement of how the claimant(s) obtained ownership of the copyright.▼

DO NOT WRITE HERE OFFICE USE ONLY

APPLICATION RECEIVED

ONE DEPOSIT RECEIVED

TWO DEPOSITS RECEIVED

REMITTANCE NUMBER AND DATE

MORE ON BACK ▶ • Complete all applicable spaces (numbers 5-9) on the reverse side of this page.
• See detailed instructions.   • Sign the form at line 8.

DO NOT WRITE HERE

Page 1 of _____ pages

DO NOT WRITE ABOVE THIS LINE. IF YOU NEED MORE SPACE, USE A SEPARATE CONTINUATION SHEET.

PREVIOUS REGISTRATION Has registration for this work, or for an earlier version of this work, already been made in the Copyright Office?
☐ Yes   ☐ No   If your answer is "Yes," why is another registration being sought? (Check appropriate box) ▼
☐ This is the first published edition of a work previously registered in unpublished form.
☐ This is the first application submitted by this author as copyright claimant.
☐ This is a changed version of the work, as shown by space 6 on this application.

If your answer is "Yes," give: **Previous Registration Number ▼**   **Year of Registration ▼**

5

DERIVATIVE WORK OR COMPILATION   Complete both space 6a & 6b for a derivative work; complete only 6b for a compilation.
a.   Preexisting Material Identify any preexisting work or works that this work is based on or incorporates. ▼

b.   Material Added to This Work Give a brief, general statement of the material that has been added to this work and in which copyright is claimed.▼

6

See instructions
before completing
this space.

DEPOSIT ACCOUNT   If the registration fee is to be charged to a Deposit Account established in the Copyright Office, give name and number of Account.
Name ▼   **Account Number ▼**

7

CORRESPONDENCE   Give name and address to which correspondence about this application should be sent.   Name/Address/Apt/City/State/Zip ▼

Area Code & Telephone Number ▶

Be sure to
give your
daytime phone
◀ number.

CERTIFICATION*   I, the undersigned, hereby certify that I am the
Check one ▼
☐ author
☐ other copyright claimant
☐ owner of exclusive right(s)
☐ authorized agent of_____
           Name of author or other copyright claimant, or owner of exclusive right(s) ▲

8

of the work identified in this application and that the statements made
by me in this application are correct to the best of my knowledge.

Typed or printed name and date ▼ If this application gives a date of publication in space 3, do not sign and submit it before that date.

_____ date ▶ _____

Handwritten signature (X) ▼

**MAIL
CERTIFI-
CATE TO**

Name ▼

Number/Street/Apartment Number ▼

City/State/ZIP ▼

**Certificate
will be
mailed in
window
envelope**

9

* 17 U.S.C. § 506(e) Any person who knowingly makes a false representation of a material fact in the application for copyright registration provided for by section 409 or in any written statement filed in connection with the application, shall be fined not more than $2,500.

December 1990—100,000

☆U.S. GOVERNMENT PRINTING OFFICE: 1990—282-170/20,006

FORM PA

UNITED STATES COPYRIGHT OFFICE

REGISTRATION NUMBER

_____

PA   PAU

EFFECTIVE DATE OF REGISTRATION

_____

Month   Day   Year

DO NOT WRITE ABOVE THIS LINE. IF YOU NEED MORE SPACE, USE A SEPARATE CONTINUATION SHEET.

1   **TITLE OF THIS WORK ▼**

PREVIOUS OR ALTERNATIVE TITLES ▼

NATURE OF THIS WORK ▼ See instructions

---

2 **a**

NAME OF AUTHOR ▼

DATES OF BIRTH AND DEATH
Year Born ▼   Year Died ▼

Was this contribution to the work a "work made for hire"?
☐ Yes
☐ No

AUTHOR'S NATIONALITY OR DOMICILE
Name of Country
OR { Citizen of ▶ _____
Domiciled in ▶ _____

WAS THIS AUTHOR'S CONTRIBUTION TO THE WORK
Anonymous? ☐ Yes ☐ No
Pseudonymous? ☐ Yes ☐ No

If the answer to either of these questions is "Yes," see detailed instructions.

NATURE OF AUTHORSHIP Briefly describe nature of the material created by this author in which copyright is claimed. ▼

NOTE

Under the law, the "author" of a "work made for hire" is generally the employer, not the employee (see instructions). For any part of this work that was "made for hire" check "Yes" in the space provided, give the employer (or other person for whom the work was prepared) as "Author" of that part, and leave the space for dates of birth and death blank.

b

NAME OF AUTHOR ▼

DATES OF BIRTH AND DEATH
Year Born ▼   Year Died ▼

Was this contribution to the work a "work made for hire"?
☐ Yes
☐ No

AUTHOR'S NATIONALITY OR DOMICILE
Name of country
OR { Citizen of ▶ _____
Domiciled in ▶ _____

WAS THIS AUTHOR'S CONTRIBUTION TO THE WORK
Anonymous? ☐ Yes ☐ No
Pseudonymous? ☐ Yes ☐ No

If the answer to either of these questions is "Yes," see detailed instructions.

NATURE OF AUTHORSHIP Briefly describe nature of the material created by this author in which copyright is claimed. ▼

c

NAME OF AUTHOR ▼

DATES OF BIRTH AND DEATH
Year Born ▼   Year Died ▼

Was this contribution to the work a "work made for hire"?
☐ Yes
☐ No

AUTHOR'S NATIONALITY OR DOMICILE
Name of Country
OR { Citizen of ▶ _____
Domiciled in ▶ _____

WAS THIS AUTHOR'S CONTRIBUTION TO THE WORK
Anonymous? ☐ Yes ☐ No
Pseudonymous? ☐ Yes ☐ No

If the answer to either of these questions is "Yes," see detailed instructions.

NATURE OF AUTHORSHIP Briefly describe nature of the material created by this author in which copyright is claimed. ▼

---

3 **a** **YEAR IN WHICH CREATION OF THIS WORK WAS COMPLETED** This information must be given in all cases.
◀ Year

b **DATE AND NATION OF FIRST PUBLICATION OF THIS PARTICULAR WORK**
Complete this information ONLY if this work has been published.
Month ▶ _____ Day ▶ _____ Year ▶ _____
◀ Nation

4

See instructions before completing this space

COPYRIGHT CLAIMANT(S) Name and address must be given even if the claimant is the same as the author given in space 2.▼

TRANSFER If the claimant(s) named here in space 4 are different from the author(s) named in space 2, give a brief statement of how the claimant(s) obtained ownership of the copyright.▼

DO NOT WRITE HERE OFFICE USE ONLY

APPLICATION RECEIVED

ONE DEPOSIT RECEIVED

TWO DEPOSITS RECEIVED

REMITTANCE NUMBER AND DATE

MORE ON BACK ▶ • Complete all applicable spaces (numbers 5-9) on the reverse side of this page.
• See detailed instructions.   • Sign the form at line 8.

DO NOT WRITE HERE

Page 1 of _____ pages

DO NOT WRITE ABOVE THIS LINE. IF YOU NEED MORE SPACE, USE A SEPARATE CONTINUATION SHEET.

PREVIOUS REGISTRATION Has registration for this work, or for an earlier version of this work, already been made in the Copyright Office?

☐ Yes ☐ No If your answer is "Yes," why is another registration being sought? (Check appropriate box) ▼

☐ This is the first published edition of a work previously registered in unpublished form.

☐ This is the first application submitted by this author as copyright claimant.

☐ This is a changed version of the work, as shown by space 6 on this application.

If your answer is "Yes," give: **Previous Registration Number ▼**   **Year of Registration ▼**

5

DERIVATIVE WORK OR COMPILATION Complete both space 6a & 6b for a derivative work; complete only 6b for a compilation.

a. **Preexisting Material** Identify any preexisting work or works that this work is based on or incorporates. ▼

b. **Material Added to This Work** Give a brief, general statement of the material that has been added to this work and in which copyright is claimed. ▼

6

See instructions
before completing
this space.

DEPOSIT ACCOUNT If the registration fee is to be charged to a Deposit Account established in the Copyright Office, give name and number of Account.

Name ▼   **Account Number ▼**

7

CORRESPONDENCE Give name and address to which correspondence about this application should be sent.   Name/Address/Apt/City/State/Zip ▼

Area Code & Telephone Number ▶

Be sure to
give your
daytime phone
◀ number

CERTIFICATION* I, the undersigned, hereby certify that I am the

Check only one ▼

☐ author

☐ other copyright claimant

☐ owner of exclusive right(s)

☐ authorized agent of_____
                Name of author or other copyright claimant, or owner of exclusive right(s) ▲

8

of the work identified in this application and that the statements made
by me in this application are correct to the best of my knowledge.

Typed or printed name and date ▼ If this application gives a date of publication in space 3, do not sign and submit it before that date.

_____ **date ▶** _____

☞ Handwritten signature (X) ▼

**MAIL
CERTIFI-
CATE TO**

Name ▼

Number/Street/Apartment Number ▼

City/State/ZIP ▼

**Certificate
will be
mailed in
window
envelope**

9

* 17 U.S.C. § 506(e) Any person who knowingly makes a false representation of a material fact in the application for copyright registration provided for by section 409, or in any written statement filed in
connection with the application, shall be fined not more than $2,500.

July 1990—135,000   ☆U.S. GOVERNMENT PRINTING OFFICE: 1990—262-308/20,001

FORM VA
UNITED STATES COPYRIGHT OFFICE

REGISTRATION NUMBER

_____

VA   VAU

EFFECTIVE DATE OF REGISTRATION

Month   Day   Year

DO NOT WRITE ABOVE THIS LINE. IF YOU NEED MORE SPACE, USE A SEPARATE CONTINUATION SHEET.

1

TITLE OF THIS WORK ▼   **NATURE OF THIS WORK ▼** See instructions

PREVIOUS OR ALTERNATIVE TITLES ▼

PUBLICATION AS A CONTRIBUTION If this work was published as a contribution to a periodical, serial, or collection, give information about the collective work in which the contribution appeared.   **Title of Collective Work ▼**

If published in a periodical or serial give: **Volume ▼**   **Number ▼**   **Issue Date ▼**   **On Pages ▼**

2

a

NAME OF AUTHOR ▼   **DATES OF BIRTH AND DEATH**
Year Born ▼   Year Died ▼

Was this contribution to the work a "work made for hire"?
☐ Yes
☐ No

AUTHOR'S NATIONALITY OR DOMICILE
Name of Country
OR { Citizen of ▶_____
Domiciled in ▶_____

WAS THIS AUTHOR'S CONTRIBUTION TO THE WORK
Anonymous? ☐ Yes ☐ No
Pseudonymous? ☐ Yes ☐ No
If the answer to either of these questions is "Yes," see detailed instructions.

NATURE OF AUTHORSHIP Briefly describe nature of the material created by this author in which copyright is claimed. ▼

NOTE

Under the law, the "author" of a "work made for hire" is generally the employer, not the employee (see instructions). For any part of this work that was "made for hire" check "Yes" in the space provided, give the employer (or other person for whom the work was prepared) as "Author" of that part, and leave the space for dates of birth and death blank.

b

NAME OF AUTHOR ▼   **DATES OF BIRTH AND DEATH**
Year Born ▼   Year Died ▼

Was this contribution to the work a "work made for hire"?
☐ Yes
☐ No

AUTHOR'S NATIONALITY OR DOMICILE
Name of country
OR { Citizen of ▶_____
Domiciled in ▶_____

WAS THIS AUTHOR'S CONTRIBUTION TO THE WORK
Anonymous? ☐ Yes ☐ No
Pseudonymous? ☐ Yes ☐ No
If the answer to either of these questions is "Yes," see detailed instructions.

NATURE OF AUTHORSHIP Briefly describe nature of the material created by this author in which copyright is claimed. ▼

c

NAME OF AUTHOR ▼   **DATES OF BIRTH AND DEATH**
Year Born ▼   Year Died ▼

Was this contribution to the work a "work made for hire"?
☐ Yes
☐ No

AUTHOR'S NATIONALITY OR DOMICILE
Name of Country
OR { Citizen of ▶_____
Domiciled in ▶_____

WAS THIS AUTHOR'S CONTRIBUTION TO THE WORK
Anonymous? ☐ Yes ☐ No
Pseudonymous? ☐ Yes ☐ No
If the answer to either of these questions is "Yes," see detailed instructions.

NATURE OF AUTHORSHIP Briefly describe nature of the material created by this author in which copyright is claimed. ▼

3

a
YEAR IN WHICH CREATION OF THIS WORK WAS COMPLETED This information must be given in all cases.
_____ ◀ Year

b
DATE AND NATION OF FIRST PUBLICATION OF THIS PARTICULAR WORK
Complete this information ONLY if this work has been published.
Month ▶_____ Day ▶_____ Year ▶_____
_____ ◀ Nation

4

See instructions before completing this space.

COPYRIGHT CLAIMANT(S) Name and address must be given even if the claimant is the same as the author given in space 2.▼

TRANSFER If the claimant(s) named here in space 4 are different from the author(s) named in space 2, give a brief statement of how the claimant(s) obtained ownership of the copyright.▼

DO NOT WRITE HERE — OFFICE USE ONLY

APPLICATION RECEIVED

ONE DEPOSIT RECEIVED

TWO DEPOSITS RECEIVED

REMITTANCE NUMBER AND DATE

MORE ON BACK ▶ • Complete all applicable spaces (numbers 5-9) on the reverse side of this page.
  • See detailed instructions.   • Sign the form at line 8.

DO NOT WRITE HERE

Page 1 of_____pages

DO NOT WRITE ABOVE THIS LINE. IF YOU NEED MORE SPACE, USE A SEPARATE CONTINUATION SHEET.

PREVIOUS REGISTRATION Has registration for this work, or for an earlier version of this work, already been made in the Copyright Office?

☐ Yes ☐ No If your answer is "Yes," why is another registration being sought? (Check appropriate box) ▼

☐ This is the first published edition of a work previously registered in unpublished form.

☐ This is the first application submitted by this author as copyright claimant.

☐ This is a changed version of the work, as shown by space 6 on this application.

If your answer is "Yes," give: **Previous Registration Number** ▼   **Year of Registration** ▼

5

DERIVATIVE WORK OR COMPILATION Complete both space 6a & 6b for a derivative work; complete only 6b for a compilation.

a. **Preexisting Material** Identify any preexisting work or works that this work is based on or incorporates. ▼

b. **Material Added to This Work** Give a brief, general statement of the material that has been added to this work and in which copyright is claimed. ▼

6

See instructions
before completing
this space.

DEPOSIT ACCOUNT If the registration fee is to be charged to a Deposit Account established in the Copyright Office, give name and number of Account.

Name ▼   **Account Number** ▼

7

CORRESPONDENCE Give name and address to which correspondence about this application should be sent. Name/Address/Apt/City/State/Zip ▼

Area Code & Telephone Number ▶

Be sure to
give your
daytime phone
◀ number.

CERTIFICATION* I, the undersigned, hereby certify that I am the

Check only one ▼

☐ author

☐ other copyright claimant

☐ owner of exclusive right(s)

☐ authorized agent of_____
      Name of author or other copyright claimant, or owner of exclusive right(s) ▲

8

of the work identified in this application and that the statements made
by me in this application are correct to the best of my knowledge.

Typed or printed name and date ▼ If this application gives a date of publication in space 3, do not sign and submit it before that date.

_____ date ▶ _____

☞ Handwritten signature (X) ▼

* 17 U.S.C. § 506(e) Any person who knowingly makes a false representation of a material fact in the application for copyright registration provided for by section 409, or in any written statement filed in connection with the application, shall be fined not more than $2,500.

December 1990—135,000

☆U.S. GOVERNMENT PRINTING OFFICE: 1990—282-170/20,007

21 Obtaining Debt Relief Through Bankruptcy

Deciding to File for Bankruptcy

The decision to file for bankruptcy is a serious one and should be given much consideration. Basically, the purpose of the bankruptcy law is to provide a means for a debtor to obtain some relief from his or her debts. Because bankruptcy can show on your credit rating for many years, you should only consider bankruptcy if no other financial solutions are available. Always do a financial analysis to see if bankruptcy is in your best interest. Seek the advice of a professional financial advisor if necessary. A helpful twelve-step program is Debtors Anonymous, which may give you insights as to how your financial difficulties can be faced without bankruptcy.

As a debtor, you normally have a choice as to the type of bankruptcy you file, and, for simple individual cases, you may file under Chapter 7 (Liquidation) or Chapter 13 (Adjustment of Debts). As an individual debtor, you can also file for reorganization of your debts under Chapter 11. Chapter 11 may be of benefit to you if you are operating a business or have unsecured debts of $100,000 or greater or secured debts of $350,000 or greater. You should consult an attorney if you are interested in filing under Chapter 11.

Liquidation may be called straight bankruptcy, and it involves the collection and distribution to creditors of all of your nonexempt property. You do keep certain exempt property. You will generally receive a discharge as to most prior debts after liquidation.

Under Chapter 13, you look for a reorganization of your debts. In a Chapter 13 case, you generally pay off your creditors through a three-year plan that is approved by the Bankruptcy Court. After payments according to the plan, you are discharged as to most prior debts and you typically retain all your property.

The filing fee at the time of this printing is $120 for Chapter 7 or Chapter 13 filings. Legal fees for a simple bankruptcy case range from about $500 to $1,000, depending on location and complexity.

Although bankruptcy cases can be complex and require legal counsel, some are simple and can be handled without an attorney. This chapter will only deal with simple, voluntary cases filed by you as an individual or jointly by you and your spouse under Chapter 7 or Chapter 13. You should be aware that involuntary cases may be filed against you by a creditor. Also, bankruptcy cases may be filed by or against a corporation or a partnership.

A bankruptcy proceeding begins with the filing of a petition with the proper Bankruptcy Court for voluntary cases. You must generally file your bankruptcy petition in the Bankruptcy Court or federal District

Court in the district where you live.

You can file for bankruptcy individually, without involving your spouse in the bankruptcy case. It is common for a husband or wife to file for bankruptcy after transferring assets to the other spouse. However, any transfers of this nature should be made more than one year before filing for bankruptcy and without intent to defraud creditors to avoid being a fraudulent transfer.

Filing under Chapter 7 — Liquidation

In filing for bankruptcy under Chapter 7, you are seeking a discharge from your debts through liquidation. There are two benefits to you in filing for bankruptcy under Chapter 7:

(1) When you file a bankruptcy petition you get immediate, but temporary, protection from collection efforts of your creditors. The filing of the bankruptcy petition automatically stops creditors from trying to collect payment from you, whether by harassing letters, telephone calls, or lawsuits to collect the debts. This relief is called a stay. The stay usually lasts until the bankruptcy proceeding is closed. However, for proper cause, a creditor may ask the Bankruptcy Court to terminate the stay.

2) A bankruptcy discharge, if granted by the court, gives you permanent relief from most, but not all, of your debts. In exchange for the discharge of debts, you will have to give up all your nonexempt property.

Filing Fee

The filing fee for a voluntary petition under Chapter 7 is currently $120. The fee is the same whether the petition is for you individually or jointly with your spouse.

The bankruptcy petition must be accompanied by the required filing fee. Checks or money orders should be made payable to "Clerk, U.S. Bankruptcy Court," or "Clerk, U.S. District Court" where applicable.

The filing fee may be paid in installments if an application for such installments is made to the Bankruptcy Court. The application for installment payment should be filed with the bankruptcy petition. The application is filed in duplicate and must be signed by you and also by your spouse if a joint petition is filed. The application should state that you are unable to pay the filing fee, except in the form of installments. The Bankruptcy Court may then permit the payment of the fee in no more than four installments. The last installment shall be paid no later than 120 days after filing. A sample Application to Pay Filing Fee In Installments (Official Form No. 2) is provided at the end of this chapter.

The Chapter 7 Bankruptcy Petition

Your case for bankruptcy under Chapter 7 is commenced by filing a bankruptcy petition with the Clerk of the Bankruptcy Court. You should use Official Form No. 1 (Debtor's Petition provided at the end of this chapter) for your individual filing. Form No. 1A (Debtor's Joint Petition provided at the end of this Chapter) should be used when filing a joint petition with your spouse. The petition should indicate that it is being filed under Chapter 7. A joint bankruptcy case is not always certain, but may be allowed by the Court for ease of administration where a husband and wife are jointly liable on their debts, and jointly hold most of their property.

There is no requirement that you be insolvent to file for bankruptcy under Chapter 7 or Chapter 13. This means that you do not have to show that you are unable to pay debts as they come due or that your liabilities are greater than your assets. The bankruptcy petition must be filed in good faith and fraudulent transfers are not permitted. The court may dismiss your case if it is an abuse of the law. There is no limit on the total amount of your debt to file a Chapter 7 case. If your financial condition indicates that you have more than enough income for necessities, you may be prohibited by the court from using Chapter 7, but may use Chapter 13 instead.

The bankruptcy petition can only be

filed by a person who resides in the United States, or has property, a domicile, or a place of business in the United States.

In the bankruptcy petition you must list your name, along with other names, maiden name, and former married name used by you within the past six years. The petition must be signed by you. In the case of a joint petition, it must be signed by both you and your spouse.

In your case filed under Chapter 7, you must file Schedules of Assets and Liabilities listing all of your debts and property. Form No. 6 provided at the end of this chapter may be used for these schedules. You must also file a Statement of Financial Affairs. Form No. 7 provided at the end of this chapter may be used for this statement i you are not engaged in a business. If you are filing a joint bankruptcy petition with your spouse, you should prepare a separate Form No. 6 and Form No.7 for your spouse, particularly if the spouse has separate assets and debts from you. You are also required to file a Schedule of Current Income and Current Expenditures (Form No. 6A). The schedules and statement of affairs should be filed along with the bankruptcy petition, although they may be filed within ten days of the bankruptcy filing. You must also provide a list of creditors with names, addresses, and zip codes. This list should be in alphabetical order and arranged in a matrix as may be required by the Bankruptcy Court.

If your schedule of assets and liabilities includes consumer debts which are secured by property that you own as collateral (such as a car, furniture or other household items), you must also file a Statement of Intentions. This statement indicates the property you plan to retain and the property you plan to surrender for your secured consumer debts.

The bankruptcy petition, along with the required schedules, statements of affairs, and creditors lists, must normally be filed in the Bankruptcy Court for the district where your domicile, place of business, or princi-

pal assets were located during the 180-day period prior to your filing for bankruptcy.

An original and three copies of the bankruptcy petition are usually required to be filed for both Chapter 7 and Chapter 13 cases. Check the specific filing requirements for your jurisdiction. You should retain a copy of all papers for your records. If you are filing a bankruptcy petition without the aid of a lawyer (*pro se*), you must file the petition in person with the Clerk of the proper Bankruptcy Court.

In a Chapter 7 bankruptcy case, you will normally have to give up all of the nonexempt property that you own at the time of filing the bankruptcy petition to be able to receive a discharge from your debts. A Bankruptcy Trustee generally collects your nonexempt property, sells it and, after taking a certain amount for the Trustee's compensation, distributes the cash to your creditors.

The Bankruptcy Trustee will also get certain property acquired by you within 180 days after filing for bankruptcy. This after-acquired property may include such things as inheritances, marital property settlements, and life insurance proceeds.

Exempt Property

Certain property and assets of yours are exempt and not involved in the bankruptcy proceeding. The kinds of property that are exempt are provided for by either state or federal law. Remember that you do not lose exempt property to the Bankruptcy Trustee. You normally have a choice of whether you would like the federal or state exemptions. Some states, however, will only allow you to claim the state exemptions. Be sure to check the exemptions and requirements for your particular state.

The federal law will allow you to claim (to the extent of any interest or equity you may have) the following as exempt property:

• Up to $7,500 in real estate or personal

property used by you or a dependent as a residence (homestead exemption), or in a burial plot for you or a dependent.

- Up to $200 per item for household furnishings, household goods, appliances, clothing, boats, books, animals, crops, or musical instruments held for personal, family, or household use; provided that the total amount of exemptions under this class can not exceed $4,000.

- Up to $500 total in jewelry held for personal, family, or household use.

- A general exemption of $400 plus up to $3,750 of any unused portion of the homestead exemption above. Thus, if you have no homestead exemption, you are allowed a general exemption of $4,150.

- Up to $750 in any books or tools of your trade or the trade of your dependent.

- Up to $1,200 in one automobile.

- Social security, unemployment, public assistance, veterans', or disability benefits.

- Payment of a pension, stock bonus, annuity, profit sharing or other similar plan, to the extent necessary for your support or the support of any dependent.

- Other miscellaneous exemptions, such as alimony, support, and certain wrongful death, insurance, and personal injury payments.

- Any property that you are claiming as exempt should be listed in Schedule B-4 of Form No. 6.

Filing under Chapter 13 — Adjustment of Debts

In filing for bankruptcy under Chapter 13 you are seeking an adjustment of your debts for a period of time according to a court approved plan. After the required payments are made according to the plan, you will receive a discharge. Unlike Chapter 7, you keep your property and assets in a Chapter 13 bankruptcy case. There is a stay of collection efforts by creditors against you and cosigners on your debts.

Filing Requirements under Chapter 13

Only certain individuals are allowed to file for bankruptcy under Chapter 13. Each individual must have an income, such as wages, a pension, social security, public assistance, or other regular payments. The individual (and his or her spouse if filing jointly) must have fixed, unsecured debts of less than $100,000 and fixed, secured debts of less than $350,000. An unsecured debt has no collateral — that is, no specific property has been set aside for the creditor to use in satisfaction of the debt if it is not paid. A secured debt does have collateral. The individual must reside in the United States or have property, a domicile, or a place of business in the United States.

The filing fee for a Chapter 13 case is currently $120.

The Chapter 13 Bankruptcy Petition

A Chapter 13 case is commenced by the filing of a bankruptcy petition with the proper Bankruptcy Court. You should use Form No. 1 for individual cases and Form No. 1A for joint cases. The petition should indicate that it is being filed under Chapter 13.

The procedures for filing the Chapter 13 petition are basically the same as for a Chapter 7 case discussed earlier. You should file Schedules of Assets and Liabilities (Form No. 6), a Chapter 13 Statement (Form No. 10), list of creditors with addresses, and a Chapter 13 Plan.

You must file a plan in a Chapter 13 case representing your best effort to make payments to creditors. The plan may not provide for payments exceeding three years, unless the court, for good cause, approves a longer period that can be no longer than five years. Under this plan, you will typically pay your income to the Bankruptcy Trustee, after you have deducted a reasonable amount for living expenses. The Trustee will then make payments to your creditors according to the plan.

The plan must provide for full payment of all priority claims such as taxes, wages, or certain undelivered or unprovided goods and services that you owe. The plan should also provide for any arrearages or back payments due on any secured debts, such as your mortgages. However, regular future payments on your secured debts should not be provided for under the plan, but should be paid outside of the plan as they are part of your regular living expenses. This is because your secured creditors are not generally affected by your Chapter 13 filing, since they can attach the collateral securing their debts if they are not paid. For example, if you have a home mortgage payment of $1,000 a month, you should treat this as part of your regular living expenses and not as a debt payment under your Chapter 13 plan. Any back payments, however, should be included in your plan to keep your secured creditors from taking foreclosure actions due to these arrearages.

In preparing your Chapter 13 plan, you should also do a separate analysis to see how your creditors would do under a Chapter 7 filing. Your Chapter 13 plan should at least provide as much satisfaction to your creditors as they would receive under a Chapter 7 case. Otherwise, your creditors may object to your plan and may be able to force you into a Chapter 7 bankruptcy.

You should start making payments under your plan within 30 days after filing. The court may dismiss your case if you do not make the required payments.

Fraudulent Transfers

If you plan to file for bankruptcy you are not permitted to transfer your property to friends and relatives or anyone else for little or no payment. Such a transfer is a fraud and will not be allowed by the Bankruptcy Court. To be fraudulent, the transfer must be done with the intent on your part to defraud your creditors or the Bankruptcy Court. If a transfer is held to be a fraudulent transfer, the creditors will be allowed to go after and recover the property that has been transferred. This usually covers all fraudulent transfers made within one year before you file for bankruptcy. Also, if the Bankruptcy Court finds that you have made a fraudulent transfer, the Court may refuse to grant a discharge to you. You are not allowed to conceal any of your property or assets.

Receiving a Discharge from Your Debts

If you receive a discharge, you are generally relieved from paying most debts that arose before your filing for bankruptcy.

A discharge from your debts is not guaranteed in a bankruptcy proceeding. However, the Bankruptcy Court will usually grant you a discharge unless the discharge is contested by your creditors or the bankruptcy trustee.

A discharge may be contested and denied to you for the following reasons:

- You have committed a fraudulent conveyance or have concealed property;

- You have falsified records, withheld records, made false claims, or attempted a bribe during the bankruptcy proceeding;

- You have refused to obey an order of the Bankruptcy Court;

- You have received a bankruptcy discharge within the past six years. Certain exceptions may apply to you for such a discharge in a prior Chapter 13 case.

In a Chapter 13 case, you usually receive a discharge after completion of the payments required under your Chapter 13 plan. In both Chapter 7 and Chapter 13 cases, the Bankruptcy Court will conduct a discharge hearing.

Nondischargeable Debts

Even if you are granted a discharge, the discharge will not apply to certain nondischargeable debts. You will still have to pay the debts that can not be discharged. The following debts will generally not be discharged through bankruptcy:

- Taxes;
- Money obtained by fraud;
- Debts not listed on Schedule (Form No. 6);
- Embezzlement or theft;
- Support and alimony;
- Fines;
- Student loans for a period of five years (discharge from a student loan may be requested after you have made payments on the loan for five years or more); and
- Debts that arise after the filing for bankruptcy.

Checklist for Filing for Bankruptcy

Chapter 7 — Voluntary Individual Liquidation

- ❏ Prepare Petition (Form No. 1 or Form No. 1A).

- ❏ Prepare Schedules of Assets and Liabilities (Form No. 6).

- ❏ Prepare Statement of Intentions indicating property that you plan to keep or surrender, if you have consumer debts which are secured by property that you own

- ❏ Prepare Statement of Financial Affairs (Form No. 7).

- ❏ Prepare Schedule of Current Income and Current Exenditures (Form No. 6A).

- ❏ Prepare List of Creditors with addresses.

- ❏ File petition, along with schedules, statements, lists, and $120 filing fee with the proper Bankruptcy Court. Obtain case number and filing date from Court Clerk.

- ❏ Attend discharge hearing and any other hearings as required by the court.

Chapter 13 — Adjustment of Debts

- ❏ Prepare Petition (Form No. 1 or Form No. 1A).

- ❏ Prepare Schedule of Assets and Liabilities (Form No. 6).

- ❏ Prepare Chapter 13 Statement (Form No. 10).

- ❏ Prepare List of Creditors with addresses.

- ❏ Prepare Chapter 13 Plan.

- ❏ File petition, along with schedules, statements, lists, and $120 filing fee with the proper Bankruptcy Court. Obtain case number and filing date from Court Clerk.

- ❏ Make payments to the Bankruptcy Trustee according to the Chapter 13 plan.

- ❏ Attend hearings as required by the court.

Using an Attorney

- ❏ Consult an attorney if your Chapter 7 or Chapter 13 bankruptcy case involves difficult or complex issues. If you check any of the items below, your case may involve complicated issues that may require legal counsel.

- ❏ Are you operating a business?

- ❏ Have you given property or assets to friends or relatives for little or no payment within the past year?

- ❏ Are you involved as a partner in a partnership?

- ❏ Have you received a bankruptcy discharge under Chapter 7 within the past six years?

- ❏ Are you a stockbroker?

- ❏ Are you filing for reorganization of your debts under Chapter 11?

Form No. 2

Application to Pay Filing Fee in Installments

United States Bankruptcy Court for the _____ District of _____

In re: _____ Case No._____

Debtor's Name_____
(Include all names used within last six years)

Social Security No._____ Telephone No._____

(Include name and Social Security No. of Debtor's spouse if a joint petition is filed.)

Applicant is filing herewith a voluntary petition under Chapter _____.

Applicant is unable to pay the filing fee except in installments.

Applicant seeks permission to pay such fees to the Clerk of the Bankruptcy Court as follows:

	Amount	Date
1.	_____	
2.	_____	
3.	_____	
4.	_____	

Applicant has paid no money and transferred no property to his/her attorney or any other person for services relative to this case or any pending bankruptcy case. Applicant will make no such payment or transfer until the filing fee is paid. Applicant certifies under penalty of perjury that the foregoing is true and correct.

Wherefore, applicant requests that he/she be permitted to pay the filing fee in installments.

Date_____ Applicant _____

Applicant _____
(Both Debtor and Spouse must sign if a joint petition is filed.)

Address _____

_____

Voluntary Case: Debtor's Petition

United States Bankruptcy Court for the _____ District of _____

In re: Case No._____

Debtor's Name_____
(Include all names used within last six years)

Social Security No._____   Telephone No._____

1. Petitioner's address is:_____

2. Petitioner has resided (or has been domiciled) in this district for the preceding 180 days (or for a longer portion of such period than in any other district).

3. Petitioner is qualified to file this petition and is entitled to the benefits of Title 11 of the United States Code as a voluntary debtor.

4. Petitioner is aware of and understands the relief available under Chapters 7, 11, 12, or 13 of Title 11, United States Code, and chooses to proceed under Chapter _____.

5. Other Declarations:

Wherefore, the petitioner respectfully requests relief in accordance with Chapter _____ of Title 11, United States Code.

I, _____, the petitioner named in the foregoing petition, certify under penalty of perjury that the foregoing is true and correct.

Date_____   Petitioner's Signature_____

Address _____

_____

Voluntary Case: Debtor's Joint Petition

United States Bankruptcy Court for the _____ District of _____

In re: Case No._____

    ❑ Debtor's Name_____

                      (Include all names used by debtor and spouse within last six years)

    ❑ Debtor's Spouse's Name_____

Debtor's Social Security No._____   Telephone No._____

Spouse's Social Security No._____

1. Petitioners' address is:_____

                                _____

2. Petitioners have resided (or have been domiciled) in this district for the preceding 180 days (or for a longer portion of such period than in any other district).

3. Petitioners are qualified to file this petition and are entitled to the benefits of Title 11 of the United States Code as a voluntary debtor.

4. Petitioners are aware of and understand the relief available under Chapters 7, 11, 12, or 13 of Title 11, United States Code, and choose to proceed under Chapter _____.

5. Other Declarations:

Wherefore, the petitioners respectfully requests relief in accordance with Chapter _____ of Title 11, United States Code.

We, _____, the petitioners

named in the foregoing petition, certify under penalty of perjury that the foregoing is true and correct.

    Date _____   Petitioner's Signature_____

                              Petitioner's Signature_____

    Address _____

               _____

Schedules of Assets and Liabilities

United States Bankruptcy Court for the _____ District of _____

In re: _____ Case No._____

Debtor's Name_____

(If a joint petition, prepare separate schedules for debtor's spouse)

Debtor's Social Security No. _____   Telephone No._____

Spouse's Social Security No. _____

These schedules are prepared for ❑ Debtor ❑ Debtor's Spouse_____(name)

Schedule A. — Statement of All Liabilities of Debtor

(Schedules A-1, A-2, and A-3 must include all the claims against the debtor, or debtor's spouse where applicable, or his/her property as of the date of the filing of the petition by or against him or her. Attach additional sheets properly identified and made a part hereof if necessary.)

Schedule A-1. - Creditors Having Priority

Nature of claim	Name of creditor and complete mailing address with zip code	Specify when claim was incurred and the consideration therefor; specify name of any part-ner or any joint contractor on any debt	Indicate if claim is con-tingent, un-liquidated, or disputed	Amount of claim
a. Wages, salary, and commissions, vacation, severance and sick leave pay owing to workmen, servants, clerks, or traveling or city salesmen on salary or commission basis, whole or part time, whether or not selling exclusively for the debtor, not exceeding $2,000 to each, earned within 90 days before filing of petition or cessation of business if earlier (specify date)				
b. Contribution to employee benefit plans for services rendered within 180 days before filing of petition or cessation of business, if earlier (specify date)				
c. Claims of farmers, not exceeding $2,000 per individual.				
d. Claims of U.S. fishermen, not exceeding $2,000 per individual.				
e Deposits by individuals, not exceeding $900 for each for purchase, lease, or rental of property or services for personal, family, or household use that was not delivered or provided				
Taxes owing (itemize) 1. To the United States 2. To any state 3. To any other taxing authority				
			TOTAL	

Schedule A-2. — Creditors holding security

Name of Creditor and complete mailing address including zip code (if unknown, so state)	Description of security and date when obtained by creditor	Specify when claim was incurred and the consideration therefor; when claim is contingent, unliquidated, disputed, or subject to setoff, evidenced by a judgment, negotiable instrument, or other writing, or incurred as partner or joint contractor, so indicate; specify name of any partner or joint contractor on any debt	Indicate if claim is contingent, unliquidated, or disputed	Market Value	Amount of claim without deduction of value of security
			TOTAL		

Schedule A-3. — Creditors having unsecured claims without priority

Name of creditor (including last known holder of any negotiable instrument) complete mailing address including zip code (if unknown, so state)	Specify when claim was incurred and the consideration therefor; when claim is contingent, unliquidated, disputed, subject to setoff, evidenced by a judgment, negotiable instrument, or other writing, or incurred as partner or joint contractor, so indicate; specify name of any partner or joint contractor on any debt	Indicate if claim is contingent, unliquidated, or disputed	Amount of claim
		TOTAL	

Schedules of Assets and Liabilities (Continued)

Schedule B. — Statement of All Property of Debtor

(Schedules B-1, B-2, B-3, and B-4 must include all property of the debtor as of the date of the filing of the petition by or against him/her. Attach additional sheets properly identified and made a part hereof, if necessary.)

Schedule B-1. — Real Property

Description and location of all real property in which debtor has an interest (including equitable and future interests, interests in estates by the entirety, community property, life estates, leaseholds, and rights and powers exercisable for his/her own behalf)	Nature of interest (specify all deeds and written instruments relating thereto)	Market value of debtor's interest without deduction for secured claims listed in Schedule A-2 or exemptions claimed in Schedule B-4
	TOTAL	

Schedule B-2. - Personal Property

Type of Property	Description and Location	Market value of debtor's interest without deduction for secured claims listed on Schedule A-2 or exemptions claimed in Schedule B-4
a. Cash on hand		
b. Deposits on money with banking institutions, savings and loan associations, credit unions, public utility companies, landlords, and others		
c. Household goods, supplies, and furnishings		
d. Books, pictures, and other art objects; stamp, coin, and other collections		
e. Wearing apparel, jewelry, firearms, sports equipment, and other personal possessions		
f. Automobiles, trucks, trailers, and other vehicles		
g. Boats, motors, and their accessories		
h. Livestock, poultry, and other animals		
i. Farming equipment, supplies, and implements		
j. Office equipment, furnishings, and supplies		
k. Machinery, fixtures, equipment, and supplies (other than those listed in Items j and l) used n business		
l. Inventory		
m. Tangible personal property of any other description		
n. Patents, copyrights, franchises, and other general intangibles (specify all documents and writings relating thereto)		
o. Government and corporate bonds and other negotiable and nonnegotiable instruments		
p. Other liquidated debts owing debtor		
q. Contingent and unliquidated claims of every nature, including counterclaims of the debtor (give estimated value of each)		
r. Interests in insurance policies (itemize surrender or refund values of each)		
s. Annuities		
t. Stock and interests in incorporated and unincorporated companies (itemize separately)		
u. Interests in partnerships		
v. Equitable and future interests, life estates, and rights or powers exercisable for the benefit of the debtor (other than those listed in Schedule B-1) (specify all written instruments relating thereto)		
	TOTAL	

Schedules of Assets and Liabilities (Continued)

Schedule B-3. — Property not otherwise scheduled

Type of Property	Description and Location	Market value of debtor's interest without deduction for secured claims listed in Schedule A-2 or exemption claimed in Schedule B-4
a. Property transferred under assignment for benefit of creditors, within 120 days prior to filing of petition (specify date of assignment, name and address of assignee, amount realized there-from by the assignee, and disposition of proceeds so far as known to debtor)		
b. Property of any kind not otherwise scheduled		
	TOTAL	

Debtor selects the following property as exempt pursuant to 11 U.S.C. 552(d) [or the laws of the State of _____]

Schedule B-4. — Property claimed as exempt

Type of Property	Location, description, and, so far as relevant to the claim of exemption, present use of property	Specify statute creating the exemption	Value claimed exempt
		TOTAL	

Schedules of Assets and Liabilities (Continued)

Summary of debts and property. (From the statement of the debtor in Schedules A and B)

Schedule	Debts	Totals
A-1/a,b	Wages, etc. having priority	
A-1(c)	Deposits of money	
A-1/d(1)	Taxes owing United States	
A-1/d(2)	Taxes owing states	
A-1/d(3)	Taxes owing other taxing authorities	
A-2	Secured claims	
A-3	Unsecured claims without priority	
	Schedule A total	

Schedule	Property	Totals
B-1	Real Property (total value)	
B-2/a	Cash on hand	
B-2/b	Deposits	
B-2/c	Household goods	
B-2/d	Books, pictures, and collections	
B-2/e	Wearing apparel and personal possessions	
B-2/f	Automobiles and other vehicles	
B-2/g	Boats, motors, and accessories	
B-2/h	Livestock and other animals	
B-2/i	Farming supplies and implements	
B-2/j	Office equipment and supplies	
B-2/k	Machinery, equipment, and supplies used in business	
B-2/l	Inventory	
B-2/m	Other tangible personal property	
B-2/n	Patents and other general intangibles	
B-2/o	Bonds and other instruments	
B-2/p	Other liquidated debts	
B-2/q	Contingent and unliquidated claims	
B-2/r	Interest in insurance policies	
B-2/s	Annuities	
B-2/t	Interests in corporations and unincorporated companies	
B-2/u	Interests in partnerships	
B-2/v	Equitable and future interests, rights, and powers	
B-3/a	Property assigned for benefit of creditors	
B-3/b	Property not otherwise scheduled	
	Schedule B total	

Unsworn Declaration under Penalty of Perjury of Individual to Schedules A and B

I, _____, certify under penalty of perjury that I have read the foregoing schedules,

consisting of _____ sheets, and that they are true and correct to the best of my knowledge, information, and belief.

Date _____   Signature _____

Statement of Financial Affairs for Debtor Not Engaged in Business

United States Bankruptcy Court for the _____ District of _____

In re: _____ Case No._____

Debtor's Name_____
(Include all names used within past six years)

Debtor's Social Security No._____ Telephone No._____

Spouse's Social Security No._____

[Each question should be answered or the failure to answer explained. If the answer is "none," or "not applicable" this should be stated. If additional space is needed for the answer to any question, a separate sheet, properly identified and made a part hereof, should be used and attached. If a joint petition, prepare a separate statement for debtor's spouse.
The term, "original petition," as used in the following questions, shall mean the petition filed under Rule 1002 or 1004.]

This statement is prepared for: ❏ Debtor   ❏ Debtor's Spouse_____(name)

1. Name and residence

a. What is your full name and social security number?

b. Have you used, or been known by, any other names within the six years immediately preceding the filing of the original petition herein? (If so, give particulars.)

c. Where do you now reside?

d. Where else have you resided during the six years immediately preceding the filing of the original petition herein?

2. Occupation and income

a. What is your occupation?

b. Where are you now employed? (Give the name and address of your employer, or the address at which you carry on your trade or profession, and the length of time you have been so employed or engaged.)

c. Have you been in a partnership with anyone, or engaged in any business during the six years immediately preceding the filing of the original petition herein? (If so, give particulars, including names, dates, and places.)

d. What amount of income have you received from your trade or profession during each of the two calendar years immediately preceding the filing of the original petition herein?

e. What amount of income have you received from other sources during each of these two years? (Give particulars, including each source and the amount received therefrom.)

3. Tax returns and refunds

a. Where did you file your federal and state income tax returns for the two years immediately preceding the filing of the original petition herein?

b. What tax refunds (income and other) have you received during the year immediately preceding the filing of the original petition?

c. To what tax refunds (income or other), if any, are you, or may you be, entitled? (Give particulars, including information as to any refund payable jointly to you and your spouse or any other person.)

4. Bank Accounts and safe deposit boxes

a. What bank accounts have you maintained, alone or together with any other person, and in your own or any other name within the two years immediately preceding the filing of the original petition herein? (Give the name and address of each bank, the name in which the deposit is maintained, and the name and address of every other person authorized to make withdrawals from such account.)

b. What safe deposit box or boxes or other depository or depositories have you kept or used for your securities, cash, or other valuables within the two years immediately preceding the filing of the original petition herein? (Give the name and address of the bank or other depository, the name in which each box or other depository was kept, the name and address of every other person who had the right of access thereto, a brief description of the contents thereof, and, if the box has been surrendered, state when surrendered, or, if transferred, when transferred, and the name and address of the transferee.)

5. Books and records

a. Have you kept books of account or records relating to your affairs within the two years immediately preceding the filing of the original petition herein?

b. In whose possession are these books or records? (Give names and addresses.)

c. If any of these books or records are not available, explain.

d. Have any books of account or records relating to your affairs been destroyed, lost, or otherwise disposed of within the two years immediately preceding the filing of the original petition herein? (If so, give particulars, including date of destruction, loss, or disposition, and reason therefor.)

6. Property held for another person

What property do you hold for any other person? (Give name and address of each person, and describe the property, or value thereof, and all writings relating thereto.)

7. Prior bankruptcy

What cases under the Bankruptcy Act or Title 11, United States Code have previously been brought by or against you? (State the location of the bankruptcy court, the nature and number of each case, the date when it was filed, and whether a discharge was granted or refused, the case was dismissed, or a composition, arrangement, or plan was confirmed.)

8. Receiverships, general assignments, and other modes of liquidation

a. Was any of your property, at the time of the filing of the original petition herein, in the hands of a receiver, trustee, or other liquidating agent? (If so, give a brief description of the property, the name and address of the receiver, trustee, or other agent, and, if the agent was appointed in a court proceeding, the name and location of the court, the title and number of the case, and the nature thereof.)

b. Have you made any assignment of your property for the benefit of your creditors, or any general settlement with your creditors, within one year immediately preceding the filing of the original petition herein? (If so, give dates, the name and address of the assignee, and a brief statement of the terms of assignment or settlement.)

9. Property in hands of third person

a. Is any other person holding anything of value in which you have an interest? (Give name and address, location and description of the property, and circumstances of the holding.)

10. Suits, executions, and attachments

a. Were you a party to any suit pending at the time of the filing of the original petition? (If so, give the name and location of the court and the title and nature of the proceeding.)

b. Were you a party to any suit terminated within the year immediately preceding the filing of the original petition herein? (If so, give the name and location of the court, the title and nature of the proceeding, and the result.)

c. Has any of your property been attached, garnished, or seized under any legal or equitable process within the year immediately preceding the filing of the original petition herein? (If so, describe the property seized or person garnished, and at whose suit.)

11. Loans repaid

What repayments on loans in whole or in part have you made during the year immediately preceding the filing of the original petition herein? (Give the name and address of the lender, the amount of the loan and when received, the amounts and dates of payments and, if the lender is a relative or insider, the relationship.)

12. Transfers of property

a. Have you made any gifts, other than ordinary and usual presents to family members and charitable donations, during the year immediately preceding the filing of the original petition herein? (If so, give names and addresses of donees and dates, description, and value of gifts.)

b. Have you made any other transfer, absolute or for the purpose of security, or any other disposition of real or tangible personal property during the year immediately preceding the filing of the original petition herein? (Give a description of the property, the date of the transfer or disposition, to whom transferred, or how disposed of, and, if the transferee is a relative or insider, the relationship, the consideration, if any, received therefor, and the disposition of such consideration.)

13. Repossessions and returns

Has any property been returned to, or repossessed by, the seller or by a secured party during the year immediately preceding the filing of the original petition herein? (If so, give particulars including the name and address of the party getting the property and its description and value.)

14. Losses

a. Have you suffered any losses from fire, thefts, or gambling during the year immediately preceding or since the filing of the original petition herein? (If so, give particulars, including dates, names, and places, and the amounts of money or value and general description of property lost.)

    b. Was the loss covered in whole or part by insurance? (If so, give particulars.)

15. Payments or transfers to attorneys

    a. Have you consulted an attorney during the year immediately preceding or since the filing of the original petition herein? (Give dates, name, and address.)

    b. Have you during the year immediately preceding or since the filing of the original petition herein paid any money or transferred any property to the attorney or to any other person on his behalf? (If so, give particulars, including amount paid or value of property transferred and date of payment or transfer.)

    c. Have you, either during the year immediately preceding or since the filing of the original petition herein, agreed to pay any money or transfer any property to an attorney at law, or to any other person on his behalf? (If so, give particulars, including amount and terms of obligation.)

I, _____, certify under penalty of perjury that I have read the answers contained in the foregoing statement of financial affairs and they they are true and correct to the best of my knowledge, information and belief.

      Date_____   Debtor's Signature _____
                                                 (or spouse's signature, if applicable)

Schedule of Current Income and Current Expenditures

United States Bankruptcy Court for the _____ District of _____

In re: Case No._____

Debtor's Name_____
(Include all names used within past six years)

Debtor's Social Security No._____ Telephone No._____

Spouse's Social Security No._____

[Complete this form by answering each question. If your answer to a question is "none" or "not applicable," so state.]

A. Family Status

1. The debtor is: [check one of the following] ❑ Married ❑ Single ❑ Separated ❑ Divorced

2. The name of the debtor's spouse is _____

3. The debtor supports the folllwing dependents [other than the debtor's spouse]:

Name	Age	Relationship to Debtor

B. Employment and Occupation

1. The debtor is employed by _____(name of employer)

    as _____(nature of position).

2. The debtor is self-employed as _____ (nature of business or profession)

    at the following principal place of business _____ (address).

3. The debtor's spouse is employed by _____(name of employer)

    as _____(nature of position).

4. The debtor's spouse is self-employed as _____ (nature of business or profession)

    at the following principal place of business _____ (address).

Schedule of Current Income and Current Expenditures (Continued)

C. Current Income

Give estimated average current monthly income of debtor and spouse, consisting of:

	Debtor	Spouse
1. Gross pay (wages, salary, or commissions)	$_____	$_____
2. Take home pay (gross pay less all deductions)	$_____	$_____
3. Regular income available from the operation of a business or profession	$_____	$_____

4. Other income:

	Debtor	Spouse
Interest and dividends	$_____	$_____
From real estate or personal property	$_____	$_____
Social Security	$_____	$_____
Pension or other retirement income	$_____	$_____
Other (specify) _____	$_____	$_____

5. Alimony, maintenance, or support payments:

	Debtor	Spouse
Payable to the debtor for the debtor's use	$_____	$_____
Payable to the debtor for the support of another (attach additional sheet listing the name, age, and relationship to the debtor of persons for whose benefit payments are made)	$_____	$_____
Total estimated current monthly income	$_____	$_____

If you anticipate receiving additional income on other than a monthly basis in the next six months (such as an income tax refund), attach additional sheet of paper and describe.

If you anticipate a substantial change in your income in the immediate future, attach additional sheet of paper and describe.

Schedule of Current Income and Current Expenditures (Continued)

D. Schedule of Current Expenditures: (give estimated average current monthly expenditures of debtor and spouse)

1. Home expenses:

   a. Rent or home loan payment (including any assessment or maintenance fee) $_____

   b. Real estate taxes $_____

   c. Utilities:

       Electricity $_____

       Gas $_____

       Water $_____

       Telephone $_____

       Other (specify)_____ $_____

               Total Utilities $_____

   d. Home maintenance (repairs and upkeep) $_____

               Total, all home expenses $_____

2. Other expenses:

   a. Taxes (not deducted from wages or included in home loan payment or included in real estate taxes) $_____

   b. Alimony, maintenance, or support payments
   (attach additional sheet listing name, age, and relationship of beneficiaries) $_____

   c. Insurance (not deducted from wages)

       Life $_____

       Health $_____

       Auto $_____

       Homeowner's or Renter's $_____

       Other (specify) _____ $_____

               Total insurance expenses $_____

   d. Installment payments:

       Auto $_____

       Other (specify) _____ $_____

   e. Transportation (not including auto payments) $_____

   f. Education (including tuition and school books) $_____

   g. Food $_____

   h. Clothing $_____

   i. Medical, dental, and medicines $_____

   j. Laundry and cleaning $_____

   k. Newspapers, periodicals, and books $_____

   l. Recreation, clubs, and entertainment $_____

   m. Charitable contributions $_____

   n. Other expenses (specify) _____ $_____

           Total estimated current monthly expenses $_____

Schedule of Current Income and Current Expenditures (Continued)

If you anticipate a substantial change in your expenses in the immediate future, attach additional sheet of paper and describe.

Unsworn Declaration under Penalty of Perjury

I/ We, _____, declare under penalty of perjury that I/We have read the foregoing schedule and any attachment, consisting of _____ sheets in all, and that they are true and correct to the best of my/our knowledge, information and belief.

Signature of Debtor _____   Date _____

Signature of Spouse_____   Date _____
                            (If joint petition, both debtors must sign.)

Chapter 13 Statement

United States Bankruptcy Court for the _____ District of _____

In re: _____ Case No._____

Debtor's Name_____
(Include all names used within past six years)

Social Security No._____ Telephone No._____

[Each question shall be answered or the failure to answer explained. If the answer is "none" or "not applicable" so state. If additional space is needed for the answer to any question, a separate sheet, properly identified and made a part hereof, should be used and attached.

The term "original petition," used in the following questions, shall mean the original petition filed under 301 of the Code or, if the Chapter 13 case was converted from another chapter of the Code, shall mean the petition by or against you which originated the first case.

This form must be completed in full whether a single or a joint petition is filed. When information is requested for "each" or "either spouse filing a petition" it should be supplied for both when a joint petition is filed. For a single petition, supply information relating only to the debtor filing the petition.]

1. Name and residence.

a. Give full name.
Husband (or if single, Debtor) _____
Wife_____

b. Where does debtor, if single, or each spouse filing a petition now reside?
(1) Mailing address of husband [or Debtor] _____
_____

(2) Mailing address of wife _____
_____

(3) Telephone number including area code: Husband [or, if single, Debtor] _____
Wife _____

c. What does debtor, if single, or each spouse filing a petition consider his or her residence, if different from that listed in b, above?
Husband [or Debtor]_____
Wife_____

2. Occupation and income.

a. Give present occupation of debtor, if single, or each spouse filing a petition. (If more than one, list all for debtor or each spouse filing a petition.)

Husband (or Debtor) _____

Wife _____

b. What is the name, address, and telephone number of present employer (or employers) of debtor, if single, or each spouse filing a petition? (Include also any identifying badge or card number with employer.)

Husband (or Debtor) _____

_____

Wife _____

_____

c. .How long has debtor, if single, or each spouse filing a petition been employed by present employer?

Husband (or Debtor) _____

Wife _____

d. If debtor or either spouse filing a petition has not been employed by present employer for a period of one year, state the name of prior employer(s) and nature of employment during that period.

Husband (or Debtor) _____

_____

Wife _____

_____

e. Has debtor or either spouse filing a petition operated a business, in partnership or otherwise, during the past three years? (If so, give the particulars, including names, dates, and places.)

Husband (or Debtor) _____

_____

Wife _____

_____

f. Answer the following questions for debtor, if single, or each spouse whether single or joint petition is filed unless spouses are separated and a single petition is filed:

(1) What are your gross wages, salary, or commissions per pay period?

	Husband (or Debtor)	Wife
(a) Weekly	_____	_____
(b) Semi-monthly	_____	_____
(c) Monthly	_____	_____
(d) Other (specify)	_____	_____

(2) What are your payroll deductions per pay period for:

(a) Payroll taxes (including social security)	_____	_____
(b) Insurance	_____	_____
(c) Credit union	_____	_____
(d) Union dues	_____	_____
(e) Other (specify)	_____	_____

(3) What is your take-home pay per pay period? _____

(4) What was the amount of your gross income
for the last calendar year? _____   _____

(5) Is your employment subject to seasonal or other change? _____   _____

(6) Has either of you made any wage assignments or allotments? [If so, indicate which spouse's wages were assigned or allotted, the name and address of the person to whom assigned or allotted, and the amount owing, if any, to such person. If allotment or assignment is to a creditor, the claim should also be listed in Item 11a.]

3. **Dependents.** (To be answered by debtor if unmarried, otherwise for each spouse whether single or joint petition is filed unless spouses are separated and a single petition is filed.)

   a. Does either of you pay (or receive) alimony, maintenance, or support? (Yes or no) _____.
   If so, how much per month?_____ For whose support? (Give name, age, and relationship to you.)

   Husband (or Debtor) _____

   _____

   Wife _____

   _____

   b. List all other dependents, other than present spouse, not listed in (a) above. (Give name, age and relationship to you.)

   Husband (or Debtor) _____

   _____

   Wife _____

   _____

4. Budget.

    a. Give your estimated average future monthly income, if unmarried,

       otherwise for each spouse whether single or joint petition is filed,

       unless spouses are separated and a single petition is filed.

         (1) Husband's [or Debtor's] monthly take-home pay   _____

         (2) Wife's monthly take-home pay   _____

         (3) Other monthly income [specify]   _____

                                                  Total   _____

    b. Give estimated average future monthly expenses of family (not including

       debts to be paid under plan), consisting of:

         (1) Rent or home mortgage payment (include lot rental for trailer)   _____

         (2) Utilities:

                Electricity   _____

                Heat   _____

                Water   _____

                Telephone   _____

                                Total Utilities   _____

         (3) Food   _____

         (4) Clothing   _____

         (5) Laundry and cleaning   _____

         (6) Newspapers, periodicals, and books (including school books)   _____

         (7) Medical and drug expenses   _____

         (8) Insurance (not deducted from wages)

                (a) Auto   _____

                (b) Other   _____

         (9) Transportation (not including auto payments to be paid under plan)   _____

         (10) Recreation   _____

         (11) Dues, union, professional, social or otherwise (not deducted from wages)   _____

         (12) Taxes (not deducted from wages)   _____

         (13) Alimony, maintenance, or support payments   _____

          (14) Other payments for support of dependents not living at home   _____

         (15) Religious and other charitable contributions   _____

         (16) Other (specify) _____   _____

                                            Total   _____

    c. Excess of estimated future monthly income over estimated future expenses

       (Total from Item 4a above minus total from Item 4b above.)   **_____**

    d. Total amount to be paid each month under plan   **_____**

5.   Payment of attorney.

    a. How much have you agreed to pay or what property have you agreed to transfer to your attorney in connection with this case?

    b. How much have you paid or what have you transferred to the attorney?

---

6.   Tax refunds. [To be answered by debtor, if unmarried, otherwise for each spouse whether single or joint petition is filed, unless spouses are separated and a single petition is filed.]

To what tax refunds (income or other), if any, is either of you, or may either of you, be entitled? [Give particulars, including information as to any refunds payable jointly to you or any other person. All such refunds should also be listed in Item 13b.]

7.   Financial accounts, certificates of deposit and safe deposit boxes. [To be answered by debtor, if unmarried, otherwise for each spouse whether single or joint petition is filed unless spouses are separated and a single petition is filed.]

    a. Does either of you currently have any accounts or certificates of deposit or shares in banks, savings and loan, thrift, building and loan and homestead associations, credit unions, brokerage houses, pension funds and the like? [If so, give name and address of each institution, number and nature of account, current balance, and name and address of every other person authorized to make withdrawals from the account. Such accounts should also be listed in Item 13b.]

    b. Does either of you currently keep any safe deposit boxes or other depositories? [If so, give name and address of bank or other depository, name and address of every other person who has a right of access thereto, and a brief description of the contents thereof, which should also be listed in Item 13b.]

8.   Prior Bankruptcy.

What cases under the Bankruptcy Act or Bankruptcy Code have previously been brought by or against you or either spouse filing a petition? (State the location of the bankruptcy court, the nature and number of each case, the date when it was filed, and whether a discharge was granted or denied, the case was dismissed, or a composition, arrangement, or plan was con firmed.)

9.   Foreclosures, executions, and attachments. (To be answered by debtor, if unmarried, otherwise for each spouse whether single or joint petition is filed unless spouses are separated and a single petition is filed.)

    a. Is any of the property of either of you, including real estate, involved in a foreclosure proceeding, in or out of court? (If so, identify the property and the person foreclosing.)

    b. Has any property or income of either of you been attached, garnished, or seized under any legal or equitable process within the 90 days immediately preceding the filing of the original petition herein? (If so, describe the property seized, or person garnished, and at whose suit.)

10. Repossessions and returns.

(To be answered by debtor, if unmarried, otherwise for each spouse whether single or joint petition is filed unless spouses are separated and a single petition is filed.)

Has any property of either of you been returned to, repossessed, or seized by the seller or by any other party, including a landlord, during the 90 days immediately preceding the filing of the original petition herein? (If so, give particulars, including the name and address of the party taking the property and its description and value.)

11. Transfers of Property.

(To be answered by debtor, if unmarried, otherwise for each spouse whether single or joint petition is filed unless spouses are separated and a single petition is filed.)

a. Has either of you made any gifts, other than ordinary and usual presents to family members and charitable donations, during the year immediately preceding the filing of the original petition herein? (If so, give names and addresses of donees and dates, description and value of gifts.)

b. Has either of you made any other transfer, absolute or for the purpose of security, or any other disposition of real or personal property during the year immediately preceding the filing of the original petition herein? (Give a description of the property, the date of the transfer or disposition, to whom transferred or how disposed of, and, if the transferee is a relative or insider, the relationship, the consideration, if any, received therefor, and the disposition of such consideration.)

12. Debts.

(To be answered by debtor, if unmarried, otherwise for each spouse whether single or joint petition is filed.)

a. Debts Having Priority.

(1) Nature of Claim	(2) Name of creditor and complete mailing address including zip code	(3) Specify when claim was incurred and the consideration there-for; when claim is is subject to setoff, evidenced by a judgment, negotiable instrument, or other writing	(4) Indicate if claim is contingent, unliquidated, or disputed	(5) Amount of claim
1. Wages, salary, and commissions, including vacation, severance and sick leave pay owing to employees not exceeding $2,000 to each, earned within ninety days before filing of petition or cessation of business (if earlier specify date.)				$_____
2. Contributions to employee benefit plans for services rendered within 180 days before filing of petition or cessation of business (if earlier specify date.)				$_____
3. Deposits by individuals, not exceeding $900 for each, for purchase, ease, or rental of property or services for personal, family, or household use that were not delivered or provided.				$_____
4. Taxes owing (itemize by type of tax and taxing authority) (A) To the United States (B) To any state (C) To any other taxing authority				$_____ $_____ $_____
			Total	$_____

b. Secured Debts. List all debts which are or may be secured by real or personal property. (Indicate in sixth column, if debt payable in installments, the amount of each installment, the installment period [monthly, weekly, otherwise] and number of installments in arrears, if any. Indicate in last column whether husband or wife is solely liable, or whether you are jointly liable.)

Creditor's name account number and complete mailing address including zip code	Consideration or basis for debt	Amount claimed by creditor	If disputed, amount admitted by debtor	Description of collateral (include year and make of automobile)	Installment amount, period and number of installments in arrears	Husband or wife, solely liable or jointly liable

Total secured debts _____

c. Unsecured Debts. List all other debts, liquidated and unliquidated, including taxes, attorney's fees, and tort claims.

Creditor's name, account number, and complete mailing address, including zip code	Consideration or basis for debt	Amount claimed by Creditor	If disputed, amount admitted by Debtor	Husband or wife solely liable, or Jointly liable

Total unsecured debts $_____

13. Codebtors. (to be answered by debtor, if unmarried, otherwise for each spouse whether single or joint petition is filed.)

  a. Are any other persons liable, as cosigners, guarantors, or in any other manner, on any of the debts of either of you or is either of you so liable on the debts of others? (If so, give particulars, indicating which spouse is liable and including names of creditors, nature of debt, names and addresses of codebtors, and their relationship, if any, to you.)

  b. If so, have the codebtors make any payments on the debts? (Give name of each codebtor and amount paid by codebtor.)

  c. Has either of you made any payments on the debts? (If so, specify total amount paid to each creditor, whether paid by husband or wife, and name of codebtor.)

14. Property and Exemptions.

(To be answered by debtor, if unmarried, otherwise for each spouse whether single or joint petition is filed.)

  a. Real Property. List all real property owned by either of you at date of filing of original petition herein. (Indicate in last column whether owned solely by husband or wife, or jointly.)

Description and location of property	Name of any coowner other than spouse	Present market value (without deduction for mortgage or other security interest)	Amount of mortgage or other security interest on this property	Name of mortgagee or other secured creditor	Value claimed exempt (specify federal or state statute creating the exemption)	Owned solely by husband or wife or jointly

b. Personal Property. List all other property, owned by either of you at date of filing of original petition herein.

Description	Location of property if not at debtor's residence	Name of coowner other than spouse	Present market value (without deduction for mortgage or other security interest)	Amount of mortgage or other security interest on this property	Name of mortgagee or other secured creditor	Value claimed exempt (specify federal or state statute creating the exemption)	Owned solely by husband or wife or jointly
Autos [give year and make]							
Household goods							
Personal effects							
Cash or financial account							
other (specify)							

(To be signed by both spouses when joint petition is filed.)

I, _____, (if joint petition is filed and I, _____,)
declare under penalty of perjury that I have read the answers contained in the foregoing statement, consisting of _____ sheets, and that they are true and complete to the best of my knowledge, information, and belief.

Husband (or Debtor) _____

Wife _____

Date _____

Chapter 13 Plan

United States Bankruptcy Court for the _____ District of _____

Debtor's Name _____ Case No _____

Spouse's Name _____

Debtor's Social Security No._____

Spouse's Social Security No. _____

1. Amount of each payment to be made by the debtor to the Bankruptcy Trustee. $_____

2. Frequency of payments. (Check one)

    ❑ Weekly   ❑ Bi-Weekly   ❑ Semi-Monthly   ❑ Monthly   ❑ Other_____

3. Amount to be paid on priority claims:

Name	Payment per Month under Plan	Total Amount to be Paid
_____	_____	_____
_____	_____	_____
_____	_____	_____

4. For secured creditors, provide the following data:

Name	Description of Collateral (Value)	Payment per Month under Plan	Total Amount to be Paid
_____	_____	_____	_____
_____	_____	_____	_____
_____	_____	_____	_____
_____	_____	_____	_____
_____	_____	_____	_____
_____	_____	_____	_____
_____	_____	_____	_____
_____	_____	_____	_____

(Attach additional sheets properly identified and made a part hereof, if necessary to complete Item 4 or 5.)

5. Amount to be paid to unsecured creditors:

Name	Payment per Month under Plan	Total Amount to be Paid
_____	_____	_____
_____	_____	_____
_____	_____	_____
_____	_____	_____
_____	_____	_____
_____	_____	_____
_____	_____	_____
_____	_____	_____

6. Bankruptcy Trustee's Compensation: $_____ per _____

7. The Plan will be completed in _____ months.

8. Other information:

Living expenses $_____ per month

Earnings and income $_____ per month

Date_____   Debtor's Signature_____

Spouse's Signature_____
(if joint petition is filed)

List of Creditors

Name:	Name:	Name:
Address:	Address:	Address:
Name:	Name:	Name:
Address:	Address:	Address:
Name:	Name:	Name:
Address:	Address:	Address:
Name:	Name:	Name:
Address:	Address:	Address:
Name:	Name:	Name:
Address:	Address:	Address:
Name:	Name:	Name:
Address:	Address:	Address:
Name:	Name:	Name:
Address:	Address:	Address:
Name:	Name:	Name:
Address:	Address:	Address:
Name:	Name:	Name:
Address:	Address:	Address:
Name:	Name:	Name:
Address:	Address:	Address:

22 *Helping You in an IRS Audit*

Dealing with the IRS

The assessment and collection of tax revenues by the federal government is an enormous undertaking and the federal government has devoted substantial resources and personnel to this task. The primary financial arm of the federal government is the Department of the Treasury. The Internal Revenue Service (IRS) is a part of the Department of the Treasury. The IRS is the agency with the responsibility of assessing and collecting federal taxes.

It is relatively easy for a taxpayer who is involved in this process to become overwhelmed by the massiveness of the United States government. However, if you are undergoing a tax audit or examination, you should approach it with calmness, sincerity, and an understanding of the assessment and collection process. This chapter will review the law and administrative procedures involved in federal tax assessment and collection and help you in dealing with the IRS.

You are entitled to courteous and considerate treatment from IRS employees at all times. If you ever feel that you are not being treated with fairness, courtesy, and consideration by an IRS employee, you should tell the employee's supervisor. You also have the right to have your tax returns kept confidential. However, if a lien or a lawsuit if filed, certain aspects of your tax case will become public records.

Most tax returns are accepted by the IRS as filed. But if your tax return is selected for audit by the IRS, it does not necessarily suggest that you are dishonest. The audit may or may not result in more taxes. Your case may be closed without change or you may receive a refund.

The Audit Process

(1) Selection of Returns

After your tax return is filed with the IRS, it is checked at the regional service center for completeness and mathematical accuracy. If a mathematical error is found, it is corrected at the service center and you are sent a correction notice of the error. If the error results in an increase in tax liability, either the refund due will be reduced accordingly or a notice and demand for payment will be sent to you. If the error results in a decrease in tax liability, you will receive a refund of that amount.

The above process should not be confused with an audit of your tax return. Any changes made to your return at this point in processing are based solely on the information contained in the tax forms and schedules. This procedure does not involve the verification of any information contained in the tax return.

Selection of most returns for audit is done through a computer program called Discriminant Function System (DFS). Under this program, tax returns are evaluated and given a score based on historical data. The scored returns are checked by IRS personnel who are called classifiers. Classifiers select those returns with the highest probability of error and then identify certain items on the selected returns for audit. For example, the classifier might select rental income and expenses, medical and interest deductions, and child care credits for examination. Other items on the selected return will not be examined unless the examining agent decides during the audit that additional items should be reviewed also.

Some returns are selected for audit under the Taxpayer Compliance Measurement Program (TCMP). This program is a random selection process to determine correct tax liability. Every four years the program is usually conducted to measure and evaluate taxpayer compliance characteristics. The next TCMP returns should be selected from the 1991 tax returns. The information obtained from these special audits is also used to update and improve the DFS system.

A TCMP audit should be distinguished from a regular audit in that the examination is not limited to a few selected items on the tax return. The audit is in depth and every item on the return is examined. Each and every income item, including exclusions of income, all exemptions and filing status, deductions, expenses, and credits are fully verified. The TCMP audits are used to generate statistical information and IRS generally does not want to drop even one audit from the sample.

Tax returns are also selected for audit through a variety of other systems. These audits may be based on information reports received by IRS from outside sources, examination of claims for refund, and through a matching of information documents. The latter system is called the Information Returns Program (IRP) in which Forms W-2, 1099, etc., are matched with the tax return to determine if all the income received has been reported on the tax return for that tax year.

(2) Audit of Your Tax Return

The audit or examination of your tax return may be conducted by correspondence, office interview, or field interview. The place and method of examination is determined by the IRS. The IRS will conduct correspondence audits only when the items shown on the tax return are very simple. Interest expenses, medical expenses, and charitable contributions are items that are commonly audited by correspondence. If your return is selected for a correspondence audit, but you would like to discuss the matter personally with an examiner, you may request a transfer of the case to the district office nearest you.

Office interviews are usually conducted by tax auditors. Tax auditors typically examine individual income tax returns which include itemized deductions, business expenses, rental income and expenses, Schedules C and F, most tax credits, and all income items. Tax auditors may also examine employment tax returns. Most of these audits are held in a local IRS office.

Field examinations are usually conducted by revenue agents and held at the taxpayer's place of business. Revenue agents typically examine individual income tax returns, partnership and corporate returns, and employment tax returns.

During a tax audit you may act on your own behalf or may be represented by an attorney, certified public accountant, by a person enrolled to practice before the IRS, or by the person who prepared the tax return and signed it as the preparer. If you filed a joint return, either you or your spouse may be present for the audit.

(3) Notification of an Audit

Notification of an audit is usually done by letter. The letter should inform you of the method of examination and, depending on the method, identify the time and place of examination, the appointment clerk or examiner's name, supervisor's name, and the office telephone number. The letter should identify those items which have been selected for audit and describe the kind of information and records needed to verify the items. The letter will also include information regarding your appeal rights and repetitive audits, both of which are discussed later.

In office examinations you are usually requested to phone the IRS office for an appointment within ten days of receipt of the notification letter. If you do not respond to the notice, the IRS may take one or more of the following actions:

- Issue a report of proposed adjustments to taxes in which all deductions for the selected items are disallowed, resulting in an increase in tax liability.

- Send you another notice by registered or certified mail.

- Issue a summons to require your presence, along with the appropriate books and records, before the examiner.

(4) What Happens During an IRS Audit?
IRS examiners are authorized to examine any books, papers, records, or memoranda bearing upon matters required to be included in your federal tax returns, to take testimony relative thereto, and to administer oaths. The examiner will generally ask pertinent questions regarding the selected items on your tax return to determine if they are allowable. If the item is allowable, the examiner will verify the amount claimed on the return. If you are unable to verify the amount claimed or if you have claimed an unallowable item, an adjustment will be made to that item. See IRS Publication 552 for recordkeeping requirements.

For example, suppose that you have claimed $100 that you gave to a neighbor whose home was destroyed by fire as a charitable contribution. Although you may be able to verify this donation through appropriate receipts, the examiner will explain that this is not an allowable deduction. To be an allowable charitable deduction the donation must be given to charitable organizations recognized by the IRS as tax-exempt organizations. Contributions to individuals, even for charitable purposes, are not deductible.

After a review of each selected item on your return, the examiner will give you the audit results and fully explain all adjustments.

Some audits may require more than one interview to close. If your records are incomplete, you may be given another opportunity to secure the necessary information. Some examinations are delayed because they require research by the examiner before a conclusion can be reached. About half of the audits conducted in office interviews by tax auditors are concluded on the first interview. However, field examinations usually take more than one interview.

Once the issues for audit have been examined, the examiner will review them with you and explain all adjustments. You should discuss each item until you are sure that you understand the reason for the adjustment. If you disagree with any adjustment you should inform the examiner of the reasons for disagreement. You may request a discussion of the issue with the examiner's group supervisor. After the discussion of the issues, the examiner will prepare a report of the audit adjustments and compute any increase or decrease in tax liability. If you agree with the adjustments you should sign the report. If you disagree with the adjustments you may exercise your appeal rights.

At the close of the audit the examiner will normally request payment of any additional taxes plus interest and any applicable penalties. Interest is computed from the due date of the tax return until the date that the tax is paid, and it fluctuates with current national interest rates. If you are unable to pay at the close of the audit, you will be billed and payment will usually be demanded within 10 days of billing. If you are due a refund as the result of the audit, you will be refunded that amount with interest. Some audits do not result in any changes to the return and the return will be accepted as filed. These audits are called "no-change" cases and you will be notified by letter when the case is closed by the examining office. Remember that an examination or audit of your tax return does not necessarily indicate that you are suspected of any dishonesty or fraud. To facilitate the entire process, you should have your records in order, request a full explanation of the audit results, and speak with the group supervisor whenever you feel this is needed.

(5) Repetitive Audits

The repetitive audit process was implemented to relieve taxpayers from repetitive audits, and the process serves both taxpayers and the Internal Revenue Service. You may qualify for repetitive audit procedures if you meet both of the following requirements:

- Your tax return was examined for the same items in either of the two previous years before the year currently under examination; and

- The previous examination resulted in no change to your tax liability or only a small change.

If you think that you meet the above requirements you should contact the person shown on the notification letter. The audit will normally be suspended pending a repetitive audit determination. If it is determined that you fall within the requirements of the repetitive audit procedures, the audit will be discontinued, unless the return was selected for audit under the Taxpayer Compliance Measurement Program.

If you have any problems that you have been unable to resolve after contacting the appropriate office, you may call or write the local IRS Problem Resolution Office. This office cannot change the tax laws or any technical decisions made by examination personnel, but it can take responsibility for other problems that arise and ensure that they receive prompt and proper attention.

Appealing an IRS Audit

If you do not agree with all or any one of the audit adjustments, you may appeal. The first step in this process is to discuss the disputed issues with the group supervisor. If the audit cannot be closed by agreement at the examination level, you may appeal within the IRS system or to the appropriate federal courts.

When you request to exercise your appeal rights the examiner will give you a report of audit adjustments, an explanation of audit adjustments, a letter notifying you of your right to appeal within thirty days from the date of the letter (thirty-day letter), and IRS Publication 5 which explains your appeal rights. If a protest letter is required in response to the thirty-day letter, it should be prepared and sent to the examiner within the thirty-day period. Protest letter requirements are discussed later. Otherwise, an oral request for an appeal normally suffices as a response to the thirty-day letter.

If you do not sign the audit agreement form or request an appeal within thirty days of the thirty-day letter, a Notice of Deficiency (ninety-day letter) will be issued. Once the ninety-day letter is issued, you generally cannot appeal within the IRS system. Rather, you must petition the United States Tax Court. If you do not petition the Tax Court within the ninety-day period, the tax will be assessed at the end of that period, and you will be billed for the tax due plus interest and any applicable penalties. If you pay the disputed tax in full, and file a claim for refund of it that is disallowed or if no action is taken by IRS within six months, then you make take your case to the U.S. District Court or the U.S. Claims Court (now part of The Court of Appeals for the Federal Circuit). In summary, you may elect any one of the following procedures if you have requested an appeal within the *thirty-day* period:

- Appeal to the Regional Appeals Office within the IRS. If you do not agree with the determination at this level, you may still take your case to the appropriate federal courts.

- Appeal to the U.S. Tax Court if the disputed issue involves income tax or certain excise taxes. You must first request that a ninety-day letter be issued to you by IRS. You have ninety days from the date of the ninety-day letter to petition the Tax Court. You may also elect to have your case heard under procedures for Small Tax Cases if the dispute does not involve more than $5,000 for any one tax year. The decisions rendered under Small Tax Case procedures are final.

- Appeal to the U.S. District Court or the U.S. Claims Court. These courts will hear cases only after the tax has been paid and a claim for refund filed. If your claim for refund is rejected by the IRS, you will receive a notice of claim disallowance. You must file suit in either federal court within two years after (a) refund claim disallowance or (b) the passage of six months after filing your claim for a refund if the IRS fails to take action on it.

Protest Letter Requirements
A formal protest letter may be required in some situations to exercise your appeal rights from an IRS audit. If a written protest letter is required, you should send it to the examiner within thirty days of the thirty-day letter. The written protest letter should include the following information:

- a statement that you wish to exercise your appeal rights;

- your name, address, and social security number;

- the date and symbols from the thirty-day letter;

- the tax periods or years involved;

- statement of the ajustments that you do not agree with;

- a statement of the facts supporting your position when the facts are in dispute; and

- a statement concerning the law or other authority upon which you are relying.

The statement of facts must also include a statement that they are true under penalty of perjury and must be signed by you.

The Collection of Unpaid Taxes
A tax assessment for unpaid taxes is generally based upon your tax return or an audit thereof. Assessments may include taxes shown on your tax returns, deficiencies in taxes, additional or delinquent taxes, and any applicable penalties and interest. Once an assessment has been made to your account by IRS, you will receive a bill which is a notice of tax due and a demand for payment. A jeopardy assessment may be made when the IRS has reason to believe that delay will jeopardize collection. In a jeopardy assessment you may be given notice with a demand for immediate payment. If you fail to pay your tax liability immediately in a jeopardy assessment, collection of the tax may be made without any additional notice.

If you cannot pay your tax liability in full, you should contact the local IRS office or the office from which you received your tax bill and explain your financial situation. You may be asked to complete a Collection Information Statement so that your financial situation can be evaluated. You may also be asked to borrow the funds or sell or mortgage assets to enable you to pay your tax liability. In addition, you may be allowed to pay your tax in installments with the amount of the installment determined by your overall financial picture.

In some cases the IRS will temporarily delay collection until you are able to pay. In such a case interest and penalties continue to accrue, since the tax debt is not forgiven. If you are entitled to a refund in subsequent tax years, it will be applied against any outstanding balance in taxes due. If you are undergoing bankruptcy proceedings, you should contact the local IRS office upon receipt of a tax bill and request a temporary stay of collection.

If you fail to pay taxes which are due, the IRS will use forced collection procedures to collect the taxes. These procedures include filing a Notice of Federal Tax Lien, serving a Notice of Levy, or seizure and sale of your property.

A tax lien is basically a claim on your property as security for the payment of taxes. Once a Notice of Federal Tax Lien is filed it becomes a public notice to all of your creditors and it also applies to any property that you acquire after filing of the notice. Total payment of the tax liability or posting of a bond will release your property from the lien.

A levy is the seizure of your property to satisfy a judgment for taxes. The tax law normally requires that the procedures below be followed before levy action can be taken:

• Assessment of tax liability;

• Submission of a tax bill to you at your last known address;

• Giving of notice of intent to levy at least ten days in advance. (The notice may be given in person, left at your residence or business, or sent by certified or registered mail to your last known address); and

• Issuance of a court order authorizing collection personnel to enter your property to take levy action.

If the IRS has reason to believe that collection may be jeopardized by delay, the ten-day waiting period and notice is waived.

Any kind of property that you own can be seized and sold to pay your tax liability, except that which is specifically exempt by the tax law. The property subject to seizure includes both personal and business property, including your personal residence. The IRS is required to give you notice of the seizure as soon as practicable. The notice must specify the sum demanded by the IRS and a description of the property to be seized. After property has been seized, the IRS will normally give you and the public notice of the proposed sale at least ten days prior to the sale of the property. The notice of sale will specify the property to be sold, the time,

place, manner, and conditions of the sale. The proceeds of levy and sale will be applied against the expenses of the proceeding and against the tax liability. Any surplus remaining after application of the proceeds as mentioned above will be credited or refunded to you, unless a creditor submits a superior claim over yours. If the proceeds of the sale are less than the tax liability, you are still responsible for the unpaid balance.

The IRS will normally release seized property before it is sold if you do one of the following:

• Pay an amount equal to the IRS' interest in the property;

• Agree to a satisfactory escrow arrangement;

• Furnish acceptable bond; or

• Make acceptable agreement for payment of the tax.

You may also redeem your property prior to the sale by paying the total amount due, including interest, penalties, and any expenses of collection. Real estate may normally be redeemed within 180 days after the sale by paying the buyer of the property the amount paid for it plus interest.

Some Useful IRS Publications

The following IRS publications may be useful to you and are available free from IRS by writing or calling **1-800-829-3676**:

Publication 1	- *Your Rights as a Taxpayer*
Publication 5	- *Appeal Rights and Preparation of Protest for Unagreed Cases*
Publication 17	- *Your Federal Income Tax*
Publication 552	- *Recordkeeping for Individuals and a List of Tax Publications*
Publication 556	- *Examination of Returns, Appeal Rights, and Claims for Refund*
Publication 586A	- *The Collection Process*
Publication 910	- *Guide to Free Tax Services*

These publications are prepared by IRS and usually give IRS' interpretation of the tax laws. If you have questions concerning IRS' views, you should consult an accountant or tax lawyer.

Appendix

Sources of Additional Information

**Administrative Office of the
United States Courts**
811 Vermont Ave., N.W. Suite 723
Washington, D.C. 20544

Allworth Press
10 E. 23rd St., Suite 400
New York, NY 10010

American Arbitration Association
140 W. 51st St.
New York, NY 10020

**American Association For
Marriage and Family Therapy**
1717 K. St., N.W. Suite 407
Washington, D.C. 20006

American Bar Association
750 N. Lake Shore Drive
Chicago, IL 60611

American Civil Liberties Union
132 W. 23rd St.
New York, NY 10109

American Marketing Association
250 S. Wacker Dr. Suite 200
Chicago, IL 60606

**Business Information Sources
University of California Press**
2120 Berkeley Way
Berkeley, CA 94704

Clark Office Products, Inc.
12750 Lake City Way, N.E.
Seattle, WA 98125

Consumer Federation of America
1424 16th St., N.W. Suite 604
Washington, D.C. 20036

Consumer Information Center
Pueblo, CO 81009

Consumer Product Safety Commission
5401 Westband Ave.
Bethesda, MD 20207

Copyright Office Library of Congress
Washington, D.C. 20559

Council of Better Business Bureaus
1515 Wilson Blvd., Suite 300
Arlington, VA 22209-3564

Directory of Business and Financial Services
1700 18th St., N.W.
Washington, D.C. 20009

**Encyclopedia of Legal Information Sources
Gale Research Co.**
645 Griswold St.
Detroit, MI 48277-0748

Federal Mediation and Conciliation Service
2100 K St., N.W.
Washington, D.C. 20037

H A L T
1319 F St., N.W. Suite 300
Washington, D.C. 20004

Handbook of Advertising & Marketing Services
919 3rd Ave., 9th Floor
New York, NY 10022-3903

Handbook of Business Finance and Capital Sources Interfinance Corp. 2
303 Blaisdell Ave.,
South Minneapolis, MN 55404

Internal Revenue Service
1111 Constitution Ave., N.W.
Washington, D.C. 20224

Legal Services Corp.
400 Virginia Ave., S.W.
Washington, D.C. 20024-2751

National Association of Realtors
430 N. Michigan Ave., Suite 500
Chicago, IL 60611

National Association of State Development Agencies
444 N. Capitol St., N.W. Suite 611
Washington, D.C. 20001

National Consumers League
815 15th St., N.W. Suite 516
Washington, D.C. 20005

National Directory of Addresses and Telephone Numbers
General Information, Inc.
401 Park Place
Kirkland, WA 98033

National Foundation for Consumer Credit
8701 Georgia Ave., Suite 507
Silver Spring, MD 20910

National Institute of Standards and Technology
Office of Energy Related Inventions
Route 270, Bldg. 202
Gaithersburg, MD 20899

National Legal Information Services
327 S. 13th St., Suite 2B
Philadelphia, PA 19107

Nolo Press
950 Parket St.
Berkeley, CA 94710

Securities and Exchange Commission
450 5th St., N.W.
Washington, D.C. 20549

Small Business Administration
1441 L St., N.W.
Washington, D.C. 20416

Society for the Right to Die
250 W. 57th St.
New York, NY 10107

The Trademark Register
National Press Bldg., Suite 1297
Washington, D.C. 20045

TRW Business Credit Services
500 City Parkway West, Suite 200
Orange, CA 92668

United States Department of Commerce
Patent and Trademark Office
Washington, D.C. 20231

United States Government Manual
Office of The Federal Register
1100 L St., N.W.
Washington, D.C. 20408

United States Government Printing Office
Superintendent of Documents
Washington, D.C. 20402

United States Information Agency
301 4th St., S.W.
Washington, D.C. 20547

Index

Acceptance of contract, 105

Administration of decedents estate, 29, 30

Affidavit, 106, 111

Affidavit of consent

    - to divorce, 87, 93

    - to name change, 101

Agent

    - for living trust, 31

    - for living will, 38

    - for power of attorney, 47, 48

    - for sale of real estate, 51

Agreement

    - Attorney's retainer agreement, 17, 18

    - Nondisclosure agreement, 117, 135

    - Lease agreement, 67, 71, 72, 73

    - Property settlement agreement, 85, 86, 89

    - Real estate agreement of sale, 52, 53, 59

    - Real estate listing agreement, 51, 52, 57

    - Trust agreement, 34, 35

Appeal

    - in small claims court, 108

    - in tax audit, 198, 199

Application

    - for copyright, 147-158

    - for patent, 122-126

    - to pay bankruptcy filing fee
        in installments, 160, 165

    - to probate will, 29, 30, 32

    - Trademark/service mark
        application, 138-140, 143

Arbitration, 104

Assignment, 43-45

    - Assignment form, 44, 45

    - Requirements for making, 43

    - Rights assignable, 43

Attorney's retainer agreement, 17, 18

Bankruptcy, 159-194

    - Adjustment of debts, 162

    - Chapter 7, 160-162

    - Chapter 13, 162

    - Checklist for filing for bankruptcy, 164

    - Discharge from debts, 160, 163

    - Exempt property, 161

    - Filing fees, 160, 162

    - Forms, 165-194

    - Fraudulent transfers, 160, 163

    - Liquidation, 160-162

    - Nondischargeable debts, 163, 164

Beneficiary

    - of a trust, 33, 34

    - of a will, 23, 24

Bill of Sale, 77-79

Capacity

    - to contract, 105

    - to make a will, 22

Closing on sale of real estate, 52, 53, 54, 55

Codicil, 23, 28

Complaint

    - Civil complaint, 105, 106, 109

    - for divorce, 87, 91

Contract (*see* also "Agreement"), 104, 105

    - contract for services, 81-84

Copyright

    - Checklist for registering a copyright, 148

    - Copyright application forms, 149-158

    - Copyright notice, 147

    - Copyright registration, 147, 148

    - Subject matter of copyright, 146, 147

Damages, 104, 105

Debts

    - Discharge through bankruptcy, 160, 163

    - Nondischargeable debts, 163, 164

Deed, 52, 55

    - General warranty deed, 55, 64

    - Quitclaim deed, 55, 66

- Special warranty deed, 55, 65

Eviction (*see* "Landlord and Tenant")

Execution of judgments, 107

Fees

- Attorney's fees, 16, 17, 23, 30, 34, 48, 51, 68, 86,
   96, 103, 118, 138, 145, 159

- Bankruptcy fees

- Copyright fees, 145

- Patent application fees, 123

- Trademark registration fees, 139, 140

Forms

- Affidavit, 111

- Assignment, 45

- Attorney's retainer agreement, 18

- Bankruptcy forms, 165-194

- Bill of Sale, 79

- Civil complaint, 109

- Codicil, 28

- Contract for Services, 83

- Copyright forms, 149-158

- Deeds, 64-66

- Divorce complaint, 91

- Lease Agreement, 73

- Living Will, 39

- Patent forms, 129-135

- Pledge of Human Body, 42

- Power of Attorney, 49

- Probate form, 32

- Promissory Note, 62

- Property settlement agreement, 89

- Real Estate forms, 57-61

- Release, 115

- Trademark form, 143

- Trust form, 35

- Will, 21

Habitability (warranty of), 69

Homestead exemption, 161

Independent contractor, 81

Infringement

- of copyrights, 146

- of patents, 127

Internal Revenue Service (*See* "Tax")

Inventions, 117-122

Judgments, 107

Landlord and Tenant, 69-75

- Assignment and subletting, 71

- Checklist for making a lease , 72

- Eviction, 70

- Forms, 73

- Obligations of landlord and tenant , 68-71

- Security deposits, 70, 71

- Types of landlord tenant relationships, 68

- Warranty of habitability, 69

Last Will and Testament

- Capacity to make, 22

- Checklist for making a will, 24

- Codicil, 23, 28

- Form, 25

- Probate, 29-32

- Requirements of a will, 21, 22, 23

- Signing of a will, 22

- Witnesses, 22, 23

Lease (*see* "Landlord and Tenant")

Living will, 37-39

Marital agreements (*see* "Property settlement")

Mortgage contingency, 52

Name

- Change of name, 95-101

Negligence, 104

Organ donor, 41, 42

Patents, 120-135

- Application for patent, 122-134

- Checklist for filing patent application, 128

- Conception and reduction to practice, 121

- Examination in Patent office, 126

- Forms, 129-135

- Infringement, 127, 128

- Patentable inventions, 121, 122

Power of attorney, 47-49

Prenuptial agreement (*see* "Property settlement")

Prepaid legal services, 16

Probate, 29-32

Promissory note, 54, 62

Property settlement, 85, 86

   - property settlement agreement, 89

Real estate, 51-66

   - Agent, 51, 52

   - Checklist for sale or purchase of

      real estate, 55, 56

   - Closing, 54, 55

   - Financing, 53, 54

   - Forms, 57-66

Registration

   - of copyrights, 145-158

   - of trademarks, 137-144

Release, 113-116

Rent (*see* "Landlord and Tenant")

Sale

   - of personal property, 77-79

   - of real estate, 51-66

Security deposits (*see* "Landlord and Tenant")

Small Claims Court, 103-111

Statute of limitations, 106

Tax, 195-200

   - Appeals, 198, 199

   - Assessments, 199

   - Audits, 195-199

   - Collection, 199, 200

   - Publications, 200

Tenant (*see* "Landlord and Tenant")

Trademarks, 137-144

   - Checklist for filing trademark application, 142

   - Classification of goods and services, 140-142

   - Form, 143

   - Function of, 137

   - Registration of, 137-144

Trial, 106, 107

Trust, 33-36

Warranty

   - Deeds, 52, 64, 65

   - of habitability in leases, 59

   - Sale of personal property, 77

Will

   - Last will and testament, 21-28

   - Living will, 37-39

Witness, 22, 23, 106,113